ISBN 978-1-397-37135-5
PIBN 11377097

LEGISLATIVE HISTORY

Public Law 85-96 -- 85th Congress

H. J. Res. 172

TABLE OF CONTENTS

Digest of Public Law 85-96

Public Law 85-96 provides that fifty thousand bales of domestically
grown extra long staple cotton in the stockpile (including any
cotton which does not meet current stockpile specifications,
established pursuant to the Strategic and Critical Materials
Stockpiling Act, as amended), shall be withdrawn and transferred
to the Commodity Credit Corporation for sale at not less than the
prices at which CCC may sell its stocks under the minimum pricing
provision of Sec. 407 of the Agricultural Act of 1949, as
amended, Proceeds from such sale, less costs incurred by CCC,
including administrative expense, as determined by the Secretary
of Agriculture, shall be covered into the Treasury of the U. S.
as miscellaneous receipts.

Jan.
17

LAW

Feb
18

mar
21

june
14

18

April
5

14

MAY

une
27

april
10

July
10

Index and Summary of History on H. J. Res. 172

January 17, 1957	H. J. Res. 172 was introduced by Rep. Rhodes and referred to House Committee on Agriculture. Print of bill as introduced.
February 18, 1957	S. J. Res. 63 was introduced by Senators Goldwater and Hayden and referred to Senate Committee on Armed Services. Print of bill as introduced.
March 21, 1957	Senate Committee on Armed Services was discharged from consideration of S. J. Res. 63 and bill was referred to Committee on Agriculture and Forestry. Print of bill as referred.
April 5, 1957	House Agriculture Committee ordered H. J. Res. 172 reported.
April 10, 1957	House Agriculture Committee reported H. J. Res. 172 without amendment. Print of bill and House Report 340.
May 6, 1957	House passed H. J. Res. 172 without amendment.
May 8, 1957	H. J. Res. 172 referred to Senate Committee on Agriculture and Forestry. Print of bill.
June 14, 1957	Senate Committee on Agriculture and Forestry ordered H. J. Res. 172 reported.
June 18, 1957	Senate Committee reported H. J. Res. 172 without amendment. Print of bill and Senate Report 463.
June 26, 1957	Senate passed over.
June 27, 1957	Senate passed without amendment. Bill as passed not printed.
July 10, 1957	Approved. Public Law 85-96.

6   rent stockpile specifications, established pursuant to the
7   Strategic and Critical Materials Stockpiling Act, as amended
8   (50 U. S. C. 98), shall be withdrawn and transferred to the
9   Commodity Credit Corporation for sale at not less than the
10   prices at which the Commodity Credit Corporation may sell
11   its stocks under the minimum pricing provision of section

I

H. J. RES. 172

IN THE HOUSE OF REPRESENTATIVES

JANUARY 17, 1957

Mr. RHODES of Arizona introduced the following joint resolution; which was referred to the Committee on Agriculture

---

JOINT RESOLUTION

Relating to the stockpile of extra long staple cotton under the Strategic and Critical Materials Stockpiling Act.

1   *Resolved by the Senate and House of Representatives*
2 *of the United States of America in Congress assembled,*
3 That notwithstanding any other provision of law, fifty thou-
4 sand bales of domestically grown extra long staple cotton in
5 the stockpile (including any cotton which does not meet cur-
6 rent stockpile specifications, established pursuant to the
7 Strategic and Critical Materials Stockpiling Act, as amended
8 (50 U. S. C. 98), shall be withdrawn and transferred to the
9 Commodity Credit Corporation for sale at not less than the
10 prices at which the Commodity Credit Corporation may sell
11 its stocks under the minimum pricing provision of section

I

1 407 of the Agricultural Act of 1949, as amended. Proceeds

2 from such sale, less costs incurred by Commodity Credit Cor-

3 poration, including administrative expense, as determined,

4 by the Secretary of Agriculture, shall be covered into the

5 Treasury of the United States as miscellaneous receipts.

85TH CONGRESS
1ST SESSION

H. J. RES. 172

JOINT RESOLUTION

Relating to the stockpile of extra-long staple cotton under the Strategic and Critical Materials Stockpiling Act.

By Mr. RHODES of Arizona

JANUARY 17, 1957

Referred to the Committee on Agriculture

stockpile specifications, established pursuant to the Strategic
6 and Critical Materials Stockpiling Act, as amended (50
8 U. S. C. 98), shall be withdrawn and transferred to the
9 Commodity Credit Corporation for sale at not less than the
10 prices at which the Commodity Credit Corporation may sell
11 its stocks under the minimum pricing provision of section

I

85TH CONGRESS
1ST SESSION

S. J. RES. 63

IN THE SENATE OF THE UNITED STATES

FEBRUARY 18, 1957

Mr. GOLDWATER (for himself and Mr. HAYDEN) introduced the following joint resolution; which was read twice and referred to the Committee on Armed Services

JOINT RESOLUTION

Relating to the stockpile of extra long staple cotton under the Strategic and Critical Materials Stockpiling Act.

1   *Resolved by the Senate and House of Representatives*

2 *of the United States of America in Congress assembled,*

3 That notwithstanding any provision of law, fifty thousand

4 bales of domestically grown extra long staple cotton in the

5 stockpile (including any cotton which does not meet current

6 stockpile specifications, established pursuant to the Strategic

7 and Critical Materials Stockpiling Act, as amended (50

8 U. S. C. 98), shall be withdrawn and transferred to the

9 Commodity Credit Corporation for sale at not less than the

10 prices at which the Commodity Credit Corporation may sell

11 its stocks under the minimum pricing provision of section

I

2

1 407 of the Agricultural Act of 1949, as amended. Proceeds
2 from such sale, less costs incurred by Commodity Credit Cor-
3 poration, including administrative expense, as determined
4 by the Secretary of Agriculture, shall be covered into the
5 Treasury of the United States as miscellaneous receipts.

85TH CONGRESS
1st Session

S. J. RES. 63

JOINT RESOLUTION

Relating to the stockpile of extra long staple
cotton under the Strategic and Critical Materials Stockpiling Act.

By Mr. GOLDWATER and Mr. HAYDEN

FEBRUARY 18, 1957

Read twice and referred to the Committee on
Armed Services

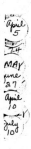

6   stockpile specifications, established pursuant to the Strategic
7   and Critical Materials Stockpiling Act, as amended (50
8   U. S. C. 98), shall be withdrawn and transferred to the
9   Commodity Credit Corporation for sale at not less than the
10 prices at which the Commodity Credit Corporation may sell
11 its stocks under the minimum pricing provision of section

I

85TH CONGRESS
1ST SESSION

S. J. RES. 63

IN THE SENATE OF THE UNITED STATES

FEBRUARY 18, 1957

Mr. GOLDWATER (for himself and Mr. HAYDEN) introduced the following joint resolution; which was read twice and referred to the Committee on Armed Services

MARCH 21, 1957

The Committee on Armed Services discharged, and referred to the Committee on Agriculture and Forestry

JOINT RESOLUTION

Relating to the stockpile of extra long staple cotton under the Strategic and Critical Materials Stockpiling Act.

1   *Resolved by the Senate and House of Representatives*

2   *of the United States of America in Congress assembled,*

3   That notwithstanding any provision of law, fifty thousand

4   bales of domestically grown extra long staple cotton in the

5   stockpile (including any cotton which does not meet current

6   stockpile specifications, established pursuant to the Strategic

7   and Critical Materials Stockpiling Act, as amended (50

8   U. S. C. 98), shall be withdrawn and transferred to the

9   Commodity Credit Corporation for sale at not less than the

10   prices at which the Commodity Credit Corporation may sell

11   its stocks under the minimum pricing provision of section

I

1 407 of the Agricultural Act of 1949, as amended.   Proceeds

2 from such sale, less costs incurred by Commodity Credit Cor-

3 poration, including administrative expense, as determined

4 by the Secretary of Agriculture, shall be covered into the

5 Treasury of the United States as miscellaneous receipts.

85TH CONGRESS
1ST SESSION

S. J. RES. 63

JOINT RESOLUTION

Relating to the stockpile of extra long staple cotton under the Strategic and Critical Materials Stockpiling Act.

By Mr. GOLDWATER and Mr. HAYDEN

FEBRUARY 18, 1957

Read twice and referred to the Committee on Armed Services

MARCH 21, 1957

The Committee on Armed Services discharged, and referred to the Committee on Agriculture and Forestry

April
5
14
MAY
june
27
april
10
July
10

CCC for sale;

H.R. 2461, providing that the level of price support for upland cotton shall be determined on the basis of the parity price for upland cotton as of June 1, prior to the beginning of the marketing year, and the supply percentage for upland cotton as of the beginning of the marketing year shall be finally determined between June 1 and June 15, inclusive.

2. HOG PRICES. Rep. Marshall stated that U. S. farmers were not receiving prices comparable to those received by Canadian farmers for meat-type hogs and that the Subcommittee on Agricultural Appropriations is looking into the matter, and inserted a statement of the Canadian Minister of Agriculture regarding the situation., p. 4645

Digest of CONGRESSIONAL PROCEEDINGS

OF INTEREST TO THE DEPARTMENT OF AGRICULTURE

OFFICE OF BUDGET AND FINANCE
(For Department Staff Only)

Issued   April 8, 1957
For actions of   April 5, 1957
85th-1st, No. 60

CONTENTS

HIGHLIGHTS: House committee ordered reported bills to revise price support for
upland cotton, extend 1956 price supports for extra long staple cotton, and sell
long staple cotton from stockpile. House committee reported Commerce appropriation bill. Rep. Marshall stated U. S. farmers receive lower hog prices than
Canadian farmers. House received GAO audit report of ACPS.

HOUSE

1. COTTON. The Agriculture Comitttee ordered reported the following bills: (p.
   D297)
        H.R. 3654, to amend the Agricultural Act of 1949 so as to continue the
   price support for extra-long staple cotton at the 1956 rate;
        H.J. Res. 172, providing for the withdrawal and transfer of 50,000 bales
   of domestically grown extra long staple cotton from the critical stockpile to
   CCC for sale;
        H.R. 2461, providing that the level of price support for upland cotton
   shall be determined on the basis of the parity price for upland cotton as of
   June 1, prior to the beginning of the marketing year, and the supply percentage
   for upland cotton as of the beginning of the marketing year shall be finally
   determined between June 1 and June 15, inclusive.

2. HOG PRICES. Rep. Marshall stated that U. S. farmers were not receiving prices
   comparable to those received by Canadian farmers for meat-type hogs and that
   the Subcommittee on Agricultural Appropriations is looking into the matter, and
   inserted a statement of the Canadian Minister of Agriculture regarding the
   situation. p. 4645

3. **PREADJOURNATIONS.** ... Committee reported ... amendment H. R. ... Committee ... agenda ... appropriation bill for 1958 (H. Rept. 30?) 465?. 4651

4. **PERSONNEL.** ... Columbia Univ. professor ... high school seniors ... 4649

Rep. ... create a separate and independent ... Appeals Office responsible to Congress (H. R. , 648?) ... active compensation to reinstated employees ... current appropriations of the agency involved (H. R. , 647?) ... dies for officers and employees who fail to comply ... recommendations of the CSC in the adjudication of veteran preference ... (H. R. 647?), 647?). 46pp. 4649-50

ELECTRIFICATION. Received ... from the ... Depar Department ... report on the ... Burns Dam, power plant ... and reservoir ... Hali project ... (HdrDoc. 193?. 147) , p. 4650

CONSERVATION. Received ... report on the ... of ACP ... for the 1958 ... fiscal year; to Government Operations Committee 465?. 4650

FOREIGN AFFAIRS. Foreign Affairs Committee issued a report pursuant to H. Res. 2 ... special study on ... Africa ... and ... of the Sahara (H. Rept. 30?)4 p. 4651
Received ... Legislature memorial ... that the 1954 Trade Agreements Act be ... to expire ... on June 30, 1958 465?. 4651

POULTRY. Received ... Legislature memorial ... establishment ... of an effective ... system ... Federal control of poultry ... handling, ... sale, ... as ... other meats. p. 465?. 4651

WATERSHED. Received ... resolution adopted by the ... the ... Watershed Assoc., Inc., advocating ... the designation of the ... Store River ... Valley, Iowa, as a pilot watershed project 465?. 4652

ADJOURNED. ... Mon., 8 ... 465?. 4650

ITEMS IN APPENDIX

11. **BUDGET.** Rep ... urging passage of ... Committee on the Budget. p. A2734

12. **WATER RESOURCES.** Rep. ... Raymond ... Upper Colp ... water resources recommendations made by ... Mississipp. A2736-A2736-7
... Rep. ... support of H. R. 6038, 6038, to construct the South ... Units Central Valley project ... noting ... support ... authorization A2763 A2743

13. **REAL ESTATE.** Rep. ... speech by the President of S. D. State ... research ... development ... for agricultural products. pp. A2739-40

14. **BUSINESS.** Rep. ... letter from a ... manufacturer of farm equipment ... business. A2740-A2740-1

3. **FEED GRAINS.** The Agriculture Committee reported without amendment H.R. 2486, to authorize the CCC to grant relief with respect to claims arising out of deliveries of eligible surplus feed grains on ineligible dates in connection with purchase orders under its emergency feed program (H. Rept. 341). p. 4917

4. **APPROPRIATIONS.** Rep. Passman criticized the transfer of requests for foreign-aid funds between agency appropriation bills and "change the name by which the foreign-aid program is identified so as to hoodwink the American people as to what the program costs". p. 4875

   The Appropriations Committee was granted permission to file, by midnight Fri., Apr. 12, reports on three appropriation bills. p. 4909

Digest of CONGRESSIONAL PROCEEDINGS

OF INTEREST TO THE DEPARTMENT OF AGRICULTURE

OFFICE OF BUDGET AND FINANCE
(For Department Staff Only)

Issued   April 11, 1957
For actions of   April 10, 1957
85th-1st, No. 63

CONTENTS

HIGHLIGHTS: Senate rejected corn bill. House concurred in Senate amendments to deferred grazing bill. Ready for President. House committee reported bills for sale of extra-long staple cotton from stockpile, and for relief from certain CCC claims on feed grain deliveries in emergency feed program. Sen. Kuchel inserted Secretary's Calif. speech.

HOUSE

1. DROUGHT RELIEF. Concurred in the Senate amendments to H.R. 2367, to establish a deferred grazing program for drought-stricken areas. This bill is now ready for the President. p. 4915

2. COTTON. The Agriculture Committee reported without amendment H.J. Res. 172, providing for the withdrawal and transfer of 50,000 bales of domestically grown extra-long staple cotton from the critical stockpile to CCC for sale (H. Rept. 340). p. 4917

3. FEED GRAINS. The Agriculture Committee reported without amendment H.R. 2486, to authorize the CCC to grant relief with respect to claims arising out of deliveries of eligible surplus feed grains on ineligible dates in connection with purchase orders under its emergency feed program (H. Rept. 341). p. 4917

4. APPROPRIATIONS. Rep. Passman criticized the transfer of requests for foreign-aid funds between agency appropriation bills and "change the name by which the foreign-aid program is identified so as to hoodwink the American people as to what the program costs". p. 4875
   The Appropriations Committee was granted permission to file, by midnight Fri., Apr. 12, reports on three appropriation bills. p. 4909

5. FLOOD CONTROL. Passed without amendment H.R. 6092, granting the consent and approval of Congress to the Merrimack River flood-control compact. pp. 4907-09

6. DEFENSE MOBILIZATION. Both Houses received from ODM a report on borrowing authority for the quarter ending Dec. 31, 1956, pursuant to sec. 304b of the Defense Production Act. pp. 4831, 4917

7. FORESTRY. Received a Comptroller General's report on the administration of forest management activities by the Bureau of Indian Affairs, Portland, Oreg., area office as of Nov. 1956. p. 4917

8. LEGISLATIVE PROGRAM. Rep. McCormack announced that H.R. 3476, to control plant pests, H.R. 5538, military land withdrawals bill, and H.R. 2146, to amend the Small Reclamation Projects Act, will be debated today. p. 4876

SENATE

9. CORN. Rejected S. 1771, to provide for a 1957 corn-base acreage of 51 million acres, by a vote of 35 ayes to 45 nays (pp. 4840-67). Sens. Hickenlooper, Thye, Humphrey, Martin, Ellender, Case of S.D., Carroll, Malone, Young, Carlson, Holland, Mundt, Aiken, Dirksen, and Potter debated the bill. Sen. Ellender inserted the Secretary's report on the present status of the corn acreage reserve program, and letters from the Farmers' Union, Farm Bureau, and the National Grange on the corn bill (pp. 4854-5); and inserted tabulations showing soil bank operations (pp. 4856-7). Sen. Potter offered an amendment to exempt producers from penalties for wheat raised and used on the farm for feed or seed, which was modified by Sen. Young limiting the referendum to farmers with allotments over 15 acres or who plant over 15 acres and excluding farmers who are exempt from quotas due to use of their entire crop for feed or seed on the farm; and the amendment was then withdrawn by Sen. Potter (pp. 4863-6). Sen. Humphrey inserted correspondence with Assistant Secretary McLain and a letter from Minn. Gov. Freeman relative to corn legislation. (pp. 4866-7).

10. FOREIGN AID. Sen. Smith, N. J., inserted Secretary of State Dulles' statement before the Special Committee to Study the Foreign Aid Program in which he urged separation of military and economic aid, and establishment of a loan fund without prior allocations by country; with an editorial of the New York Times supporting the proposal. pp. 4838-40

11. PERSONNEL. Began consideration of S. 1832, to authorize the appointment of an additional Assistant Secretary of State, which became its unfinished business. pp. 4831, 4867/8
As reported (see Digest 61) S. 385, to authorize the training of Federal employees at public or private facilities, provides as follows:
That appropriations or other funds available for salaries or expenses shall also be available for authorized training; that tuition, fees, and similar related expenses may be paid to the training institution or to the trainee; that no agency funds shall be available to pay for training at any facility that teaches or advocates the overthrow of the Government of the United States by force or violence; that no training shall be provided under the bill for any employee unless authorized by the head of the agency or his duly designated representative; that regulations pursuant to the bill shall be issued by the President and shall set forth obligations to which employees given training under the bill shall agree; that any trainee failing to fulfil these obligations shall be required to reimburse the Government for the expense of the training to the extent the head of the agency finds equitable; that

RELEASE OF STOCKPILED LONG STAPLE COTTON

APRIL 10, 1957.—Committed to the Committee of the Whole House on the State
of the Union and ordered to be printed

Mr. COOLEY, from the Committee on Agriculture, submitted the
following

REPORT

[To accompany H. J. Res. 172]

The Committee on Agriculture, to whom was referred the joint
resolution (H. J. Res. 172) relating to the stockpile of extra long staple
cotton under the Strategic and Critical Materials Stockpiling Act,
having considered the same, report favorably thereon without amendment and recommend that the joint resolution do pass.

PURPOSE OF BILL

The purpose of this bill is to require the release from the strategic
and critical materials stockpile of 50,000 bales of domestic extra long
staple cotton and the sale of such cotton into regular commercial
channels by the Commodity Credit Corporation. Under the provisions of the Agricultural Act of 1949 referred to in the resolution,
the minimum price at which CCC could sell this cotton would be
105 percent of the current support price plus carrying charges.
Actually, the cotton would probably sell somewhat above this price.
Extra long staple cotton is a relatively new crop in the United
States and although production has increased substantially in the
past few years, domestic production still falls short of domestic consumption. The growers of this type of cotton have staged an aggressive merchandizing campaign and have developed a substantial
market for their commodity in this country. As part of this merchandizing campaign, they have sought to keep the price of extra long
staple cotton at levels low enough to compete successfully with
foreign-produced extra long staple cotton and with other fibers. In
this connection, the committee has recently reported a bill (H. R.
3654) which will prevent the support level on extra long staple cotton
from going up, as it very likely would otherwise do, under the flexible
pricing provisions of the Agricultural Act of 1949.

86006

9   Commodity Credit Corporation for sale at not less than the

10   prices at which the Commodity Credit Corporation may sell

11   its stocks under the minimum pricing provision of section

I

facility that teaches or advocates the overthrow of the Government of the
United States by force or violence; that no training shall be provided under
the bill for any employee unless authorized by the head of the agency or his
duly designated representative; that regulations pursuant to the bill shall
be issued by the President and shall set forth obligations to which employees
given training under the bill shall agree; that any trainee failing to fulfil
these obligations shall be required to reimburse the Government for the expense
of the training to the extent the head of the agency finds equitable; that

---

2   RELEASE OF STOCKPILED LONG STAPLE COTTON

Substantial quantities of this cotton have been placed in the critical
materials stockpile. It has been known for some time that the
quantity in the stockpile exceeded the stockpile goal and only recently
the Office of Defense Mobilization has made a determination that
this type of cotton is no longer a critical material. At the same time
supplies of this cotton in the United States have become quite short,
and the producers are fearful that the tight supply situation, combined with price increases which inevitably occur under such supply
situations, will cause some of those now using this cotton to turn to
other fibers and deprive the long staple cotton producers of part of
the market they have succeeded in building up.

For this reason, the producers consider it urgent that the amount
of cotton covered by this resolution be released from the stockpile
immediately so that it can be made available to the trade in the period
between now and the harvest next fall of this year's cotton crop.
Particularly in view of the recent action of ODM, there appears to the
committee to be no reason why this should not be done.

DEPARTMENTAL VIEWS

The following letter from the Department of Agriculture sets out in
more detail reasons for enactment of this legislation at this time.

DEPARTMENT OF AGRICULTURE,
Washington, D. C., April 9, 1957.

Hon. HAROLD D. COOLEY,
Chairman, Committee on Agriculture,
House of Representatives.

DEAR CONGRESSMAN COOLEY: This is in reply to your request of
March 13, 1957, for a report on House Joint Resolution 172, a joint
resolution relating to the stockpile of extra long staple cotton under
the Strategic and Critical Materials Stockpiling Act.

From the standpoint of the responsibilities of this Department,
enactment of the proposed legislation would be beneficial. However,
we are not in a position to comment on the foreign policy implications
of the proposal.

This joint resolution provides that notwithstanding any provision
of law, 50,000 bales of domestically grown extra long staple cotton
in the stockpile (including any cotton which does not meet current
stockpile specifications, established pursuant to the Strategic and
Critical Materials Stockpiling Act, as amended) shall be withdrawn
and transferred to the Commodity Credit Corporation for sale at
not less than the prices at which the Commodity Credit Corporation
may sell its stocks under the minimum pricing provision of section
407 of the Agricultural Act of 1949, as amended.

Proceeds from such sale, less costs incurred by CCC, including
administrative expense, as determined by the Secretary of Agriculture,
shall be covered into the Treasury of the United States as miscellaneous receipts.

It is generally agreed by those familiar with the stockpile operations
that the current inventory of extra long staple cotton in the stockpile
is somewhat larger than is considered necessary to meet the needs for
which it was obtained. On this basis, it is our position that at least
50,000 bales can be released from the stockpile, as proposed in the bill,
without adversely affecting our supply situation. Since the quantity

of extra long staple cotton in the stockpile is classified information, representatives of this Department will be available to meet with the Committee on Agriculture for any further discussion of the matter which may be considered necessary.

The cotton in the stockpile was acquired at prices averaging about $1.05 a pound. The price at which this cotton could now be sold under the provisions of the bill is approximately 63 cents a pound.

The loss to the Government on 50,000 bales, if it were now withdrawn and sold, would be about $10,500,000. Storage on such cotton is costly to the Government, however, and if the quantity specified is not presently needed, it would be better to dispose of it and take the loss in order to avoid further storage expense.

Your attention is invited to the fact that on March 13, 1957, Mr. Arthur S. Flemming, Director, Office of Defense Mobilization, notified Mr. Franklin G. Floete, Administrator, General Services Administration, that his Office had determined, pursuant to section 2 (a) of the Strategic and Critical Materials Stockpiling Act, that (1) extra long staple cotton should be removed from the current list of strategic and critical materials for stockpiling and (2) the stockpile inventory of extra long staple cotton should be sold in accordance with section 3 (e) of the act. We do not believe this action should interfere with enactment by the Congress of House Joint Resolution 172. The stockpile of extra long staple cotton contains substantially more than 50,000 bales; however, even if the executive and legislative branches have no differences of opinion on the plans formulated for selling the entire stockpile of cotton and they can be developed without delay, it will be near the end of the year before any of the cotton could be made available for sale because section 3 (e) of the act requires the disposal plan to be published in the Federal Register and filed with the Congress for 6 months prior to the beginning of execution of the plan. The 50,000 bales covered by the bill are needed to meet demand that exists now and most likely will continue until the new domestic crop is harvested beginning in October.

The Bureau of the Budget advises that there is no objection to the submission of this report.

Sincerely yours,

MARVIN L. McLAIN,
Assistant Secretary.

5

9 Commodity Credit Corporation for sale at not less than the

10 prices at which the Commodity Credit Corporation may sell

11 its stocks under the minimum pricing provision of section

5. FLOOD CONTROL.
   approval of (
   09

6. DEFENSE MOBILI
   authority for
   Defense Produ

7. FORESTRY. Rec
   forest manage
   area office a

8. LEGISLATIVE PF
   pests, H.R. 5
   Small Reclam

9. CORN. Rejecte
   acres, by a v
   Thye, Humphre
   Carlson, Noll
   Sen. Ellender
   corn acreage
   Bureau, and t
   tabulations a
   an amendment
   the farm for
   referendum to
   and excluding
   crop for feec
   Sen. Potter (
   Secretary McI
   lation. (pp.

10. FOREIGN AID.
    before the Sp
    separation of
    without prior
    supporting th

11. PERSONNEL. Be
    additional As
    pp. 4831, 486
         As repo
    employees at
         That ap
    shall also be
    similar/relat
    trainee; that

85TH CONGRESS
1ST SESSION
H. J. RES. 172

[Report No. 340]

IN THE HOUSE OF REPRESENTATIVES

JANUARY 17, 1957

Mr. RHODES of Arizona introduced the following joint resolution; which was referred to the Committee on Agriculture

APRIL 10, 1957

Committed to the Committee of the Whole House on the State of the Union and ordered to be printed

---

JOINT RESOLUTION

Relating to the stockpile of extra long staple cotton under the Strategic and Critical Materials Stockpiling Act.

1   *Resolved by the Senate and House of Representatives*
2 *of the United States of America in Congress assembled,*
3 That notwithstanding any other provision of law, fifty thou-
4 sand bales of domestically grown extra long staple cotton in
5 the stockpile (including any cotton which does not meet cur-
6 rent stockpile specifications) established pursuant to the
7 Strategic and Critical Materials Stockpiling Act, as amended
8 (50 U. S. C. 98), shall be withdrawn and transferred to the
9 Commodity Credit Corporation for sale at not less than the
10 prices at which the Commodity Credit Corporation may sell
11 its stocks under the minimum pricing provision of section

I

2

1 407 of the Agricultural Act of 1949, as amended. Proceeds

2 from such sale, less costs incurred by Commodity Credit Cor-

3 poration, including administrative expense, as determined

4 by the Secretary of Agriculture, shall be covered into the

5 Treasury of the United States as miscellaneous receipts.

Union Calendar No. 105

85TH CONGRESS
1ST SESSION

H. J. RES. 172

[Report No. 340]

JOINT RESOLUTION

Relating to the stockpile of extra long staple cotton under the Strategic and Critical Materials Stockpiling Act.

By Mr. RHODES of Arizona

JANUARY 17, 1957

Referred to the Committee on Agriculture

APRIL 10, 1957

Committed to the Committee of the Whole House on the State of the Union and ordered to be printed

Office of the Secretary, increased costs resulting from Federal Pay
   Act of 1956, $23,400.
Forest Service, control of forest pests, $800,000.
(All of the above amounts are the same as the Budget Estimates and would
 be provided by transfer from other appropriations of the Department.)
Increase in administrative expense limitation for Commodity Credit
   Corporation, $2,000,000 (Budget Estimate, $2,500,000).
Various amounts for claims for damages, audited claims, and judgments.
Excerpts from the committee report:
   Emergency range conservation. "The committee has not included budget
   language which would have permitted the transfer of $25,000,000 from funds
   available to the Soil Bank to implement the recommendations on deferred

J

Digest of CONGRESSIONAL PROCEEDINGS

OF INTEREST TO THE DEPARTMENT OF AGRICULTURE

OFFICE OF BUDGET AND FINANCE
(For Department Staff Only)

Issued   May 7, 1957
For actions of   May 6, 1957
85th-1st, No. 74

CONTENTS

HIGHLIGHTS: House passed bills for sale of extra-long staple cotton from stockpile
and for relief from certain CCC claims in emergency feed program. Rep. Coad
criticized administration of farm program. House committee reported (May 3) third
supplemental appropriation bill. House committee ordered reported bills to extend
Public Law 480, to provide compulsory inspection of poultry, and to provide self-
help meat promotion program.

HOUSE - May 3

1. THIRD SUPPLEMENTAL APPROPRIATION BILL, 1957. The Appropriations Committee
   reported without amendment this bill, H.R. 7221, (H. Rept. 386). p. 5710
   The bill includes the following items for this Department:
     Agricultural Research Service:
       Increase of $66,000 in limitation on construction of buildings for
       replacement of a building at the Big Spring (Tex.) Field Station.
       Penalty mail costs of State Experiment Station Directors, $250,000.
       Federal Extension Service, penalty mail costs of State Extension Service
       Directors, $514,000.
       Office of the Secretary, increased costs resulting from Federal Pay
       Act of 1956, $23,400.
       Forest Service, control of forest pests, $800,000.
       (All of the above amounts are the same as the Budget Estimates and would
       be provided by transfer from other appropriations of the Department.)
       Increase in administrative expense limitation for Commodity Credit
       Corporation, $2,000,000 (Budget Estimate, $2,500,000).
     Various amounts for claims for damages, audited claims, and judgments.
   Excerpts from the committee report:
     Emergency range conservation. "The committee has not included budget
     language which would have permitted the transfer of $25,000,000 from funds
     available to the Soil Bank to implement the recommendations on deferred

grazing in the President's recent drought message. New legislation on this subject has just been adopted which will require the submission of a revised estimate at a later date. The Committee feels that this item should be denied at this time. Also, it is to be noted that the situation has now changed in much of the drought area."

'Employees' life insurance. "The Committee has not approved a $76,500 increase in limitation for administrative expenses of this fund. The amount was requested for the Federal Government to assume the assets and liabilities of certain employee beneficial associations. Approval would cost the insurance fund $22,000,000. The Committee is sympathetic, however, to the insurance needs of members of associations who retired from Federal employment before the Federal insurance program became effective, and would consider a fair and reasonable by the Civil Service Commission to assume the policies of such members."

Flood insurance. "The committee has denied the $50,000,000 budget estimate to institute a new and experimental subsidy program of Federal flood insurance, but recommends that the agency use the $325,000 it now has for further study to develop a more workable plan. The proposal for flood indemnity that has been presented to the Committee is too indefinite and costly.

"The present plan contemplates that 40% of the cost of the premiums and all administrative costs would be borne by the Federal government. The premium cost is almost prohibitive. The Government would underwrite all losses, and estimates of those losses are too indefinite. The program certainly would be very costly to the Government and the policyholders.

"It is clear that the budget estimate for $50,000,000 is merely the initial step committing the taxpayers to a new program and the Committee does not recommend such a step at this time when every effort is being made to reduce Federal spending."

HOUSE - May 6

2. COTTON. Passed without amendment H. J. Res. 172, to provide for the transfer of 50,000 bales of extra-long staple cotton from the _stockpile_ to _CCC_ for sale at not less than the prices which CCC may sell its own stocks. p. 5666

3. FEED GRAINS. Passed without amendment H.R. 2486, to authorize _CCC_ to grant relief with respect to claims arising out of deliveries of eligible surplus feed grains on ineligible dates in connection with purchase orders under the emergency feed program. p. 5666

4. FARM PROGRAM. Rep. Coad criticized farm policies as being favorable to the "large, efficient commercial farmers," and urged the appointment of former Congressman Clifford Hope as Secretary of Agriculture. pp. 5660-61

5. SURPLUS DISPOSAL; POULTRY; MEATS. The Agriculture Committee ordered reported, on May 3, the following bills: p. D375

   H.R. 6974, to extend the Agricultural Trade Development and Assistance Act of 1954 (Public Law 480) for one year, to increase the authorization under Title I from $3 billion to $4 billion, and to authorize $300 million additional under Title II for famine relief.

   H.R. 6814, to provide for the compulsory inspection by the Department of Agriculture of poultry and poultry products.

   H.R. 5244 (a clean bill to be introduced), to provide for a self-help meat promotion program.

Mr. Speaker, House Joint Resolution 230 that is really before the House now for consideration and which is House Calendar No. 43 is as follows:

Resolved, etc., That service or employment of any person not presently employed by the Federal Government as an attorney, accountant, expert, or professional staff member in assisting the Committee on Ways and Means of the House of Representatives, or any duly authorized subcommittee thereof, in the investigations authorized by House Resolution 104, 85th Congress, shall not be considered as service or employment bringing such person within the provisions of section 281, 283, or 284 of title 18 of the United States Code, or of any other Federal law imposing restrictions, requirements, or penalties in relation to the employment of persons, the performance of services, or the payment or receipt of compensation in connection with any claim, proceeding, or matter involving the United States.

It will be noticed that this House Joint Resolution 230 refers to House Resolution 104. That resolution is as follows:

Resolved, That, effective from January 4, 1957, the Committee on Ways and Means, acting as a whole or by subcommittee, is authorized to conduct through studies and investigations of all matters coming within the jurisdiction of such committee.

Sec. 2. For the purpose of this resolution, the committee, or any subcommittee thereof, is authorized to hold such hearings, to sit and acting during the present Congress at such times and places, within the continental United States, its Territories, and possessions, as the committee may determine, whether, or not the House has recessed, or has adjourned, to require the attendance of such witnesses and the production of such books, papers, and documents by subpena or otherwise, to administer such oaths, and to take such testimony, as it deems necessary. Subpenas may be issued under the signature of the chairman of the committee or of any subcommittee, or by any member designated by any such chairman, and may be served by any person designated by any such chairman or member.

Sec. 3. The committee may report to the House at any time during the present Congress the results of any studies or investigations made under authority of this resolution, together with such recommendations as it deems appropriate. Any such report which is made when the House is not in session shall be filed with the Clerk of the House.

It will also be noticed that if this resolution, House Joint Resolution 230, is passed, it will allow all the personnel selected by the House Committee on Ways and Means to have the exemption provided in the resolution. In other words, it will not be confined to one subcommittee that happens to be investigating tariff matters. The resolution will provide exemptions for all employees working for the Committee on Ways and Means or any subcommittee thereof in the investigation authorized by Resolution 104.

The committee's report clearly outlines the objective of the proposed exemption from the conflict-of-interest statutes. It is as follows:

The Committee on the Judiciary, to whom was referred the joint resolution (H. J. Res. 230) to suspend the application of certain Federal laws with respect to personnel employed by the House Committee on Ways and Means in connection with the investigations ordered by House Resolution 104, 85th Congress, having considered the same, report

favorably thereon without amendment and recommend that the joint resolution do pass.

PURPOSE OF THE LEGISLATION

The purpose of this resolution is to suspend the application of certain Federal laws—the so-called conflict-of-interest statutes contained in sections 281, 283, and 284 of title 18 of the United States Code—with respect to personnel to be employed by the House Committee on Ways and Means in connection with the investigations authorized by House Resolution 104, 85th Congress.

GENERAL STATEMENT

House Resolution 104 authorized the Ways and Means Committee of the House of Representatives to conduct studies and investigations of all matters coming within the jurisdiction of that committee. In order to assist the committee in carrying out its legislative responsibility, it has been found necessary to employ experts. Understandably, it has been found increasingly difficult to induce professional men to accept such committee assignments. Under the present law, such assignments preclude persons so employed from appearing for profit before Government agencies and bureaus. Moreover, the ban would continue for 2 years after termination of such employment over matters which an individual may have handled while employed by the Government.

In the past, many resolutions similar to this have been enacted and are, therefore, precedents for the enactment of this resolution.

It should also be pointed out that these restrictions and limitations of the present law affect individuals who merely serve on a temporary basis. Unless exemptions like those embodied in this resolution are granted, the House Committee on Ways and Means will be deprived of the specific talents and ability of outstanding men and women essential to the work of the committee, since such persons will not wish to forfeit their right to practice for profit before a governmental bureau or agency.

Therefore, the Committee on the Judiciary recommends the favorable enactment of this resolution:

The following are the specific sections of title 18 of the United States Code which would be waived by the enactment of this resolution.

EXISTING LAW

TITLE 18. UNITED STATES CODE

§ 281. Compensation to Members of Congress, officers and others in matters affecting the Government

"Whoever, being a Member of or Delegate to Congress, or a Resident Commissioner, either before or after he has qualified, or the head of a department, or other officer or employee of the United States or any department or agency thereof, directly or indirectly, receives or agrees to receive, any compensation for any services rendered or to be rendered, either by himself or another, in relation to any proceeding, contract, claim, controversy, charge, accusation, arrest, or other matter in which the United States is a party or directly or indirectly interested, before any department, agency, court martial, officer, or any civil, military, or naval commission, shall be fined not more than $10,000 or imprisoned not more than 2 years, or both; and shall be incapable of holding any office of honor, trust, or profit under the United States.

"Retired officers of the Armed Forces of the United States, while not on active duty, shall not by reason of their status as such be subject to the provisions of this section. Nothing herein shall be construed to allow any retired officer to represent any person in the sale of anything to the Government through the department in whose service he holds a retired status.

"This section shall not apply to any person because of his membership in the National Guard of the District of Columbia nor to any person especially excepted by act of Congress.

"§ 283. Officers or employees interested in claims against the Government

"Whoever, being an officer or employee of the United States or any department or agency thereof, or of the Senate or House of Representatives, acts as agent or attorney for prosecuting any claim against the United States, or aids or assists in the prosecution or support of any such claim otherwise than in the proper discharge of his official duties, or receives any gratuity, or any share of or interest in any such claim in consideration of assistance in the prosecution of such claim, shall be fined not more than $10,000 or imprisoned not more than 1 year, or both.

"This section shall not apply to any person because of his membership in the National Guard of the District of Columbia nor to any person specially excepted by enactment of Congress.

"§ 284. Disqualifications of former officers and employees in matters connected with former duties

"Whoever, having been employed in any agency of the United States, including commissioned officers assigned to duty in such agency, within 2 years after the time when such employment or service has ceased, prosecutes or acts as counsel, attorney, or agent for prosecuting, any claims against the United States involving any subject matter directly connected with which such person was so employed or performed duty, shall be fined not more than $10,000 or imprisoned not more than 1 year, or both."

The first three lines of the language of the report are:

Suspending the application of certain Federal laws with respect to personnel employed by the House Committee on Ways and Means.

So there is no attempt to mislead anyone, and I am certainly not charging any bad faith.

I am shocked to think that the House would consider without any debate, by unanimous consent, adopt such an unusual and far-reaching bill. It should come up under a rule. When the Revenue Act of 1954 passed the House of Representatives, it was under a gag rule. We were told that it was so involved that very few Members knew what the bill contained; many of them on the committee did not know all of its provisions. We were told that it was prepared by the experts.

After this bill became law, it was discovered there were some very large loopholes in it. In fact, the Government is losing tens of millions of dollars, possibly billions of dollars a year by reason of these enormous loopholes that were never discovered, when the bill was being considered in Congress. We know that the bill is largely the work of experts. The shocking thing is that we will have experts who are actually engaged in the practice of law and who can profit the most from loopholes in tax laws to be actually allowed to help write them for the Congress.

Furthermore, we say in the resolution that even if an employee of the committee engages in a conspiracy against the Government and uses his position as an employee to feather his own nest and to allow his client great profit, that he will not be punished because we are exempting him in advance from any law that would cause him to be punished.

It does not make sense to me. I will have to get more convincing information before agreeing to this proposal.

The SPEAKER. Is there objection to the present consideration of the bill?

Mr. PATMAN. Mr. Speaker, I ask unanimous consent that the bill may be passed over without prejudice.

The SPEAKER. Is there objection to the request of the gentleman from Texas?

There was no objection.

RELINQUISHMENT OF OFFICE OF CHIEF JUDGE

The Clerk called the bill (H. R. 985) to provide that chief judges of circuit and district courts shall cease to serve as such upon reaching the age of 70.

Mr. ROGERS of Colorado. Mr. Speaker, I ask unanimous consent that this bill may be passed over without prejudice.

The SPEAKER. Is there objection to the request of the gentleman from Colorado?

There was no objection.

RELEASE OF STOCKPILED LONG STAPLE COTTON

The Clerk called the resolution (H. J. Res. 172) relating to the stockpile of extra long staple cotton under the Strategic and Critical Materials Stockpiling Act.

There being no objection, the Clerk read the resolution, as follows:

Resolved, etc., That notwithstanding any other provision of law, 50,000 bales of domestically grown extra long staple cotton in the stockpile (including any cotton which does not meet current stockpile specifications) established pursuant to the Strategic and Critical Materials Stockpiling Act, as amended (50 U. S. C. 98), shall be withdrawn and transferred to the Commodity Credit Corporation for sale at not less than the prices at which the Commodity Credit Corporation may sell its stocks under the minimum pricing provision of section 407 of the Agricultural Act of 1949, as amended. Proceeds from such sale, less costs incurred by Commodity Credit Corporation, including administrative expense, as determined by the Secretary of Agriculture, shall be covered into the Treasury of the United States as miscellaneous receipts.

The resolution was ordered to be engrossed and read a third time, was read the third time, and passed, and a motion to reconsider was laid on the table.

EMERGENCY FEED PROGRAM

The Clerk called the bill (H. R. 2486) to authorize Commodity Credit Corporation to grant relief with respect to claims arising out of deliveries of eligible surplus feed grains on ineligible dates in connection with purchase orders under its emergency feed program.

There being no objection, the Clerk read the bill, as follows:

Be it enacted, etc., That Commodity Credit Corporation, under such regulations as may be approved by the Secretary of Agriculture, is hereby authorized to grant relief to farmers and dealers in connection with claims arising out of early and late deliveries under purchase orders for drought relief feed issued under the 1954, 1955, and 1956 emergency feed programs, by recognizing as valid those purchases and deliveries of designated surplus feed grains and approved mixed feeds, which (a) were actually purchased by the farmer from the dealer on or after the date the Secretary declared the county, where the purchase order was issued, to be eligible for assistance under the emergency feed program, and (b) are found to have been physically delivered to the farmer not later than 12 months from the date the purchase order was issued to the farmer.

The bill was ordered to be engrossed and read a third time, was read the third time and passed, and a motion to reconsider was laid on the table.

DESIGNATION OF JIM WOODRUFF DAM AS LAKE SEMINOLE

The Clerk called the bill (H. R. 3077) providing that the lake created by the Jim Woodruff Dam on the Apalachicola River located at the confluence of the Flint and Chattahoochee Rivers be known as Lake Seminole.

There being no objection, the Clerk read the bill, as follows:

Be it enacted, etc., That the lake created by the Jim Woodruff Dam on the Apalachicola River located at the confluence of the Flint and Chattahoochee Rivers in southwest Georgia shall be known and designated as Lake Seminole in honor of the Seminole Indians whose ancestors, the Richiti's and Apalachicola's, inhabited the general area in which this lake is located. Any law, regulation, document, or record of the United States in which such lake is referred to under any other name or designation, shall be held to refer to such lake as Lake Seminole.

The bill was ordered to be engrossed and read a third time, was read the third time and passed, and a motion to reconsider was laid on the table.

ADJUSTING PENALTIES RELATING TO INJURIOUS NONMAILABLE MATTER

The Clerk called the bill (H. R. 4193) to amend section 1716 of title 18, United States Code, so as to conform to the act of July 14, 1956 (70 Stat. 538–540).

There being no objection, the Clerk read the bill, as follows:

Be it enacted, etc., That section 1716 of title 18, United States Code, as amended, is further amended by striking out the words "3 years" in the seventh paragraph, and by inserting in lieu thereof, the words "1 year"; by striking out the words "10 years" in the eighth paragraph and by inserting in lieu thereof the words "20 years"; and by adding a new paragraph to read as follows:

"Whoever is convicted of any crime prohibited by this section, which has resulted in the death of any person, shall be subject also to the death penalty or to imprisonment for life, if the jury shall in its discretion so direct, or, in the case of a plea of guilty, or a plea of not guilty where the defendant has waived a trial by jury, if the court in its discretion, shall so order."

(Mr. KEATING asked and was given permission to extend his remarks at this point in the RECORD.)

Mr. KEATING. Mr. Speaker, last year 44 persons were killed on a commercial airliner, which blew up over Colorado after a bomb had been placed aboard. This tragic occurrence led me to introduce a bill to prescribe the death penalty for such willful destruction of aircraft or motor vehicles. That bill became Public Law 709 in the 84th Congress.

In my opinion, it is as serious an offense to send a bomb through the mails as it is to place one aboard an aircraft. H. R. 4193 would, in effect, extend the provisions of Public Law 709 to cases where death or injury resulted from depositing outlawed objects in the mails with intent to kill or injure others.

The need for such legislation has been illustrated by a number of instances over the past 20 years in which innocent persons, including employees of the Post Office Department, have been killed or severely injured by explosives. At the present time the perpetrator of a crime as heinous as this is subject, under Federal law, only to a fine of not more than $10,000 or to imprisonment for not more than 10 years, or both.

Mr. Speaker, it is time we acted to prevent tragedies, such as have occurred in the past, by increasing the penalty to fit the crime.

The bill was ordered to be engrossed and read a third time, was read the third time, and passed, and a motion to reconsider was laid on the table.

VALIDATING OVERPAYMENTS WHILE AT CIVILIAN HOSPITALS

The Clerk called the bill (H. R. 3366) to validate overpayments of pay and allowances made to certain officers of the Army, Navy, Naval Reserve, and Air Force, while undergoing training at civilian hospitals, and for other purposes.

There being no objection, the Clerk read the bill, as follows:

Be it enacted, etc., That notwithstanding any other law, all payments of pay and allowances made to any commissioned officer of the Medical Corps of the Army, Navy, or the Naval Reserve, or any medical officer of the Air Force, who, while serving on active duty before July 1, 1954, as an intern or resident physician in a hospital other than a Federal hospital, received compensation from that hospital (including meals and living quarters in kind), are validated to the extent that such pay and allowances were paid.

SEC. 2. Any person covered by section 1 who has made a repayment to the United States of the amount so paid to him as pay or allowances is entitled to be paid the amount involved, if otherwise proper. Any repayment hereby authorized will be made from appropriations currently available for pay and allowances.

SEC. 3. In the audit and settlement of the accounts of any certifying or disbursing officer full credit shall be given for the amount for which liability is relieved by this act.

The bill was ordered to be engrossed and read a third time, was read the third time and passed, and a motion to reconsider was laid on the table.

7 Strategic and Critical Materials Stockpiling Act, as amended
8 (50 U. S. C. 98), shall be withdrawn and transferred to the
9 Commodity Credit Corporation for sale at not less than the
10 prices at which the Commodity Credit Corporation may sell
11 its stocks under the minimum pricing provision of section

I

the third time, and passed, and a motion to reconsider was laid on the table.

EMERGENCY FEED PROGRAM

The Clerk called the bill (H. R. 2486) to authorize Commodity Credit Corporation to grant relief with respect to claims arising out of deliveries of eligible surplus feed grains on ineligible dates in connection with purchase orders under its emergency feed program.

There being no objection, the Clerk read the bill, as follows:

Be it enacted, etc., That Commodity Credit Corporation, under such regulations as may be approved by the Secretary of Agriculture, is hereby authorized to grant relief to farmers "2 years" in the seventh paragraph, and by inserting in lieu thereof, the words "1 year"; by striking out the words "10 years" in the eighth paragraph and by inserting in lieu thereof the words "20 years"; and by adding a new paragraph to read as follows:

"Whoever is convicted of any crime prohibited by this section, which has resulted in the death of any person, shall be subject also to the death penalty or to imprisonment for life, if the jury shall in its discretion so direct, or, in the case of a plea of guilty, or a plea of not guilty where the defendant has waived a trial by jury, if the court in its discretion, shall so order."

(Mr. KEATING asked and was given permission to extend his remarks at this point in the RECORD.)

paid.

SEC. 2. Any person covered by section 1 who has made a repayment to the United States of the amount so paid to him as pay or allowances is entitled to be paid the amount involved, if otherwise proper. Any repayment hereby authorized will be made from appropriations currently available for pay and allowances.

SEC. 3. In the audit and settlement of the accounts of any certifying or disbursing officer full credit shall be given for the amount for which liability is relieved by this act.

The bill was ordered to be engrossed and read a third time, was read the third time and passed, and a motion to reconsider was laid on the table.

H. J. RES. 172

IN THE SENATE OF THE UNITED STATES

MAY 8, 1957

Read twice and referred to the Committee on Agriculture and Forestry

JOINT RESOLUTION

Relating to the stockpile of extra long staple cotton under the Strategic and Critical Materials Stockpiling Act.

1 *Resolved by the Senate and House of Representatives*
2 *of the United States of America in Congress assembled,*
3 That notwithstanding any other provision of law, fifty thou-
4 sand bales of domestically grown extra long staple cotton in
5 the stockpile (including any cotton which does not meet cur-
6 rent stockpile specifications) established pursuant to the
7 Strategic and Critical Materials Stockpiling Act, as amended
8 (50 U. S. C. 98), shall be withdrawn and transferred to the
9 Commodity Credit Corporation for sale at not less than the
10 prices at which the Commodity Credit Corporation may sell
11 its stocks under the minimum pricing provision of section

I

1 407 of the Agricultural Act of 1949, as amended.   Proceeds
2 from such sale, less costs incurred by Commodity Credit Cor-
3 poration, including administrative expense, as determined
4 by the Secretary of Agriculture, shall be covered into the
5 Treasury of the United States as miscellaneous receipts.

Passed the House of Representatives May 6, 1957.

Attest: RALPH R. ROBERTS,
                                    Clerk.

85TH CONGRESS
1st Session

H. J. RES. 172

JOINT RESOLUTION

Relating to the stockpile of extra long staple cotton under the Strategic and Critical Materials Stockpiling Act.

MAY 8, 1957

Read twice and referred to the Committee on Agriculture and Forestry

the th
to reco

EN
The
to aut
tion to
arising
feed g
tion
emerg
The
read t
Be it
Corpor
be app
is here

reported S. 1521, to exempt student trainee appointees from the Civil Service provision prohibiting the employment of more than two members of a family in the classified service. p. D531

5. FARM POLICY. The Subcommittee on Agricultural Policy of the Joint Economic Committee announced that it had selected Dr. George E. Brandow as staff economist to conduct its forthcoming study of agricultural policy. p. D532

6. LEGISLATIVE PROGRAM. Rep. McCormack announced that the Consent Calendar will be called Mon., June 17, to be followed during this week with consideration of H.R. 6974, to extend Public Law 480; H.R. 7221, the conference report on the

une th
to rec

EA
The
to aut
tion to
arising
feed g
tion
emerg
The
read t
Be th
Corpor
be app
is here

Digest of CONGRESSIONAL PROCEEDINGS

OF INTEREST TO THE DEPARTMENT OF AGRICULTURE

OFFICE OF BUDGET AND FINANCE
(For Department Staff Only)

Issued   June 17, 1957
For actions of   June 14, 1957
85th-1st, No. 103

CONTENTS

HIGHLIGHTS: Senate passed mutual security bill. Senate committee ordered reported bills to release extra long staple cotton for stockpile, to modify relation of supports on burley and Virginia tobacco, to exempt certain wheat producers from marketing penalties, and to transfer wheat acreage allotments of lands taken by right of eminent domain. Sen. Smith, N.J., introduced and discussed bills to establish Senior Civil Service, improve employment practices, and create Advisory Council of Health.

HOUSE

1. APPROPRIATIONS. Conferees were appointed on H.R. 6500, the D.C. appropriation bill for 1958 (p. 8109). Senate conferees were appointed June 11.

2. HOUSING. Conferees were appointed on H.R. 6659, the housing bill (p. 8109). Senate conferees were appointed May 29.

3. AREA REDEVELOPMENT. Rep. Lane spoke in favor of legislation to assist local distressed areas in economic redevelopment. pp. 8147-48

4. PERSONNEL. A subcommittee of the Post Office and Civil Service Committee ordered reported S. 1521, to exempt student trainee appointees from the Civil Service provision prohibiting the employment of more than two members of a family in the classified service. p. D531

5. FARM POLICY. The Subcommittee on Agricultural Policy of the Joint Economic Committee announced that it had selected Dr. George E. Brandow as staff economist to conduct its forthcoming study of agricultural policy. p. D532

6. LEGISLATIVE PROGRAM. Rep. McCormack announced that the Consent Calendar will be called Mon., June 17, to be followed during this week with consideration of H.R. 6974, to extend Public Law 480; H.R. 7221, the conference report on the

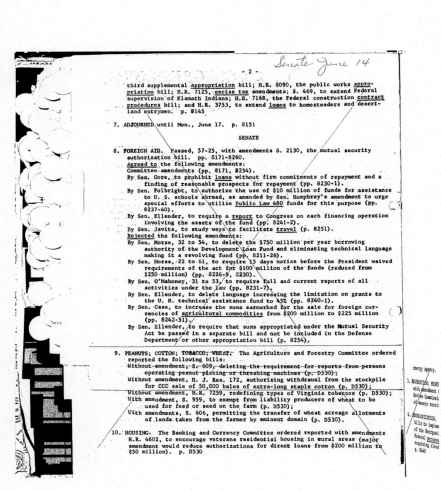

Senate — June 14

third supplemental appropriation bill; H.R. 8090, the public works appropriation bill; H.R. 7125, excise tax amendments; S. 469, to extend Federal supervision of Klamath Indians; H.R. 7168, the Federal construction contract procedures bill; and H.R. 3753, to extend loans to homesteaders and desert-land entrymen. p. 8145

7. ADJOURNED until Mon., June 17. p. 8151

SENATE

8. FOREIGN AID. Passed, 57-25, with amendments S. 2130, the mutual security authorization bill. pp. 8171-8260.
   Agreed to the following amendments:
   Committee amendments (pp. 8171, 8254).
   By Sen. Gore, to prohibit loans without firm commitments of repayment and a finding of reasonable prospects for repayment (pp. 8230-1).
   By Sen. Fulbright, to authorize the use of $10 million of funds for assistance to U. S. schools abroad, as amended by Sen. Humphrey's amendment to urge special efforts to utilize Public Law 480 funds for this purpose (pp. 8237-40).
   By Sen. Ellender, to require a report to Congress on each financing operation involving the assets of the fund (pp. 8241-2).
   By Sen. Javits, to study ways to facilitate travel (p. 8251).
   Rejected the following amendments:
   By Sen. Morse, 32 to 54, to delete the $750 million per year borrowing authority of the Development Loan Fund and eliminating technical language making it a revolving fund (pp. 8211-26).
   By Sen. Morse, 22 to 61, to require 15 days notice before the President waived requirements of the act for $100 million of the funds (reduced from $250 million) (pp. 8226-9, 8230).
   By Sen. O'Mahoney, 31 to 53, to require full and current reports of all activities under the law (pp. 8231-7).
   By Sen. Ellender, to delete language increasing the limitation on grants to the U. N. technical assistance fund to 45% (pp. 8240-1).
   By Sen. Case, to increase the sums earmarked for the sale for foreign currencies of agricultural commodities from $200 million to $225 million (pp. 8242-51).
   By Sen. Ellender, to require that sums appropriated under the Mutual Security Act be passed in a separate bill and not be included in the Defense Department or other appropriation bill (p. 8254).

9. PEANUTS; COTTON; TOBACCO; WHEAT. The Agriculture and Forestry Committee ordered reported the following bills:
   Without amendment, S. 609, deleting the requirement for reports from persons operating peanut picking or threshing machines (p. D530);
   Without amendment, H. J. Res. 172, authorizing withdrawal from the stockpile for CCC sale of 50,000 bales of extra-long staple cotton (p. D530);
   Without amendment, H.R. 7259, redefining types of Virginia tobaccos (p. D530);
   With amendment, S. 959, to exempt from liability producers of wheat to be used for feed or seed on the farm (p. D530);
   With amendments, S. 606, permitting the transfer of wheat acreage allotments of lands taken from the farmer by eminent domain (p. D530).

10. HOUSING. The Banking and Currency Committee ordered reported with amendments H.R. 4602, to encourage veterans residential housing in rural areas (major amendment would reduce authorizations for direct loans from $200 million to $50 million). p. D530

energy agency.

3. RECREATION; MINES with amendment t Review Commissic of moneys receiv

4. REORGANIZATION. bills to implem of the Reorgani Federal personne requiring clear p. 8440

Energy Agency. pp. 8447-8, 8449-50, 8451-68, 8491-8508, 8509-24, 8525-34

3. RECREATION; MINERALS. The Interior and Insular Affairs Committee ordered reporte
   with amendment S. 846, to establish a National Outdoor Recreation Resources
   Review Commission, and without amendment H.R. 3477, relating to the disposition
   of moneys received from mineral lands in Alaska. p. D542

4. REORGANIZATION. Received the President's message urging enactment of certain
   bills to implement recommendations of the Hoover Commission, including extension
   of the Reorganization Act of 1949, accrued expenditure appropriations, training
   Federal personnel at private or public facilities, and repeal of provisions
   requiring clearance of real property transactions with Congressional committees.
   p. 8440

without amendment; 3. buy; deleting the requirement for reports from persons

Digest of CONGRESSIONAL PROCEEDINGS

OF INTEREST TO THE DEPARTMENT OF AGRICULTURE

OFFICE OF BUDGET AND FINANCE
(For Department Staff Only)

Issued   June 19, 1957
For actions of   June 18, 1957
85th-1st, No. 105

CONTENTS

HIGHLIGHTS: House adopted conference report on third supplemental appropriation bill. House debated public works appropriation bill. House committee ordered reported bills to permit soil bank lands to be used in establishing future acreage allotments, and to remove green peanuts from marketing penalties. House received proposed health insurance plan to establish Outdoor Recreation Resources Commission. Senate committee ordered reported bill to release extra-long staple cotton from stockpile. Sen. Clark introduced and discussed bill to establish commission to study and revise pay system for Federal employees.

SENATE

1. COTTON. The Agriculture and Forestry Committee reported without amendment H.J. Res. 172, authorizing removal from the strategic stockpile for CCC sale of 50,000 bales of extra long staple cotton (S. Rept. 463). p. 843

2. ATOMIC ENERGY. Ratified as reported the Statute of the International Atomic Energy Agency. pp. 8447-8, 8449-50, 8451-68, 8491-8508, 8509-24, 8525-34

3. RECREATION; MINERALS. The Interior and Insular Affairs Committee ordered reporte with amendment S. 846, to establish a National Outdoor Recreation Resources Review Commission, and without amendment H.R. 3477, relating to the disposition of moneys received from mineral lands in Alaska. p. D542

4. REORGANIZATION. Received the President's message urging enactment of certain bills to implement recommendations of the Hoover Commission, including extension of the Reorganization Act of 1949, accrued expenditure appropriations, training Federal personnel at private or public facilities, and repeal of provisions requiring clearance of real property transactions with Congressional committees. p. 8440

5. HOUSING. The Banking and Currency Committee reported with amendments H.R. 4602, to encourage residential housing for veterans in rural areas (S. Rept. 464). p. 8443

6. ELECTRIFICATION; LOANS. S. 555, the Hells Canyon dam bill, was made the Senate's unfinished business. p. 8534
Sen. Humphrey inserted a resolution favoring Hells Canyon high dam from the Carlton County, Minn., Cooperative Power Assn. p. 8442
Sen. Humphrey inserted a Carlton County, Minn., Cooperative Power Assn. resolution urging that the interest rate for REA loans to cooperatives not be increased. pp. 8442-3

7. FLOOD INSURANCE. Sen. Bush inserted an editorial urging appropriations for the Federal Flood Indemnity Administration. pp. 8446-7

8. STUDENT EXCHANGE. Sen. Fulbright inserted an editorial and two letters on the value of the international student-exchange program. p. 8447

9. PERSONNEL. Sen. Humphrey expressed his gratification over the pay-raise bill reported to the Senate Post Office and Civil Service Committee by Sen. Neuberger's subcommittee, and inserted his letter to the Senator. p. 8448

10. FISCAL POLICY. Sens. Humphrey, Bush, McNamara, Case of S.D., Long, Capehart, Carlson, Lausche, Holland, Fulbright, and Wiley discussed the Administration's fiscal and monetary policies and their effect on the economy, and Sen. Bush inserted Treasury Secretary Humphrey's statement before the Senate Finance Committee on the financial condition of the U.S. (pp. 8482-90). pp. 8468-90

11. WATER RESOURCES. Sen. Johnson stated that without the multi-purpose projects the recent floods in Texas would have cost $100 million more, and urged the value of flood control and water conservation projects. pp. 8439-40

12. FOOD DISTRIBUTION. Received a Calif. Legislature resolution urging positive steps to stockpile surplus foods in Calif. for civil defense. pp. 8440-1

13. IMPORTS. Received a Calif. Legislature resolution urging limitations on the import of dried figs and fig paste. p. 8441

14. LANDS. Received a Calif. Legislature resolution urging the lease of lands near Parker Dam to the Parker Dam County Recreation District. p. 8441

15. WHEAT. Sen. Carlson inserted a Woodlawn, Kans., Farmers' Union resolution urging a 'yes' vote on the wheat marketing quota referendum to be held June 20. p. 8443

HOUSE

16. APPROPRIATIONS. Adopted the conference report on H.R. 7221, the third supplemental appropriation bill for 1957 (pp. 8546-73). Agreed to provide $4 million (instead of $15 million as proposed by the Senate), to remain available through June 30, 1958, for emergency conservation measures (p. 8547) and $11,500,000 (instead of $15,000,000 as proposed by the Senate) for emergency feed and seed assistance (p. 8548). Rejected, 186 to 218, a motion by Rep. Boland to agree to the Senate amendment providing $14,000,000 for a Federal flood insurance program (pp. 8548-6Q). This bill now goes to the Senate for consideration. (For other items of interest see Digest 88.)

JUNE 18, 1957.—Ordered to be printed

Mr. EASTLAND, from the Committee on Agriculture and Forestry,
submitted the following

REPORT

[To accompany H. J. Res. 172]

The Committee on Agriculture and Forestry, to whom was referred
the joint resolution (H. J. Res. 172) relating to the stockpile of extra
long staple cotton under the Strategic and Critical Materials Stockpiling Act, having considered the same, report thereon with a recom-
mendation that it do pass without amendment.

The joint resolution provides for the transfer to, and sale by, Commodity Credit Corporation of 50,000 bales of extra long staple cotton
now in the stockpile established pursuant to the Strategic and Critical
Materials Stock Piling Act. The Office of Defense Mobilization
recently concluded that present inventories of long staple cotton
should be sold; but the Stock Piling Act requires 6 months' notice
prior to sale. The effect of the joint resolution will therefore be to
waive the 6-month delay with regard to 50,000 bales.

Section 3 (e) of the Stock Piling Act, which provides for the 6-month
notice, provides further that the date of disposition shall be fixed with
due regard to the protection of the United States against avoidable
loss on the sale and with due regard to the protection of producers,
processors, and consumers against avoidable disruption of their usual
markets. Due at least in part to Egypt's decision to sell a substantial
portion of its crop to Russia, a shortage of long staple cotton has
developed. The new crop will not be available until October and there
is some danger that consumers may be forced to switch to other fibers
or other markets before the new crop becomes available. If producers,
processors, and consumers are to be protected, and if the United States
loss is to be kept to the minimum, the cotton should be made available
now, while the shortage exists rather than after the new crop becomes
available. The Department of State and the Office of Defense Mobilization have suggested that Egypt and other long staple producing
countries should be able to rely on the 6-month notice provision, but
your committee believes that foreign as well as domestic producers

86008

the

ves

'ed,

ou-

in

ur-

the

led

the

the

10   prices at which the Commodity Credit Corporation may sell

11   its stocks under the minimum pricing provision of section

would be best protected by sale of this cotton during the current shortage before consumers are forced to turn to other sources of fiber.

Section 301 (d) of the Agricultural Adjustment Act of 1938 provides as follows:

> (d) In making any determination under this Act or under the Agricultural Act of 1949 with respect to the carryover of any agricultural commodity, the Secretary shall exclude from such determination the stocks of any commodity acquired pursuant to, or under the authority of, the Strategic and Critical Materials Stock Piling Act (60 Stat. 596; 7 U. S. C. 1301 (d)).

So long as this cotton remains in the stockpile it is clear that it would not be counted as part of the carryover, even though it were available for sale under section 3 of the Stock Piling Act. However, some question has arisen as to whether the provision of the joint resolution that the cotton be "withdrawn and transferred to the Commodity Credit Corporation" would remove this cotton from the provision of section 301 (d). There is no such intention. The cotton would remain subject to section 301 (d) whether held by one agency of the Government or another and will not be counted as part of the carryover so long as it is held by the Commodity Credit Corporation.

The Department of Agriculture advised on April 9 that the cotton in the stockpile was acquired at prices averaging about $1.05 a pound, and could then be sold at about 63 cents a pound for a loss of about $10,500,000. Since then the price has weakened somewhat, so that prompt passage of the bill is needed to avert further loss. Passage of the joint resolution will therefore result in no increase in expenditures, but will reduce expenditures for storage charges and avert further loss.

The report of the House Committee on Agriculture on this joint resolution and reports from the Department of State and the Office of Defense Mobilization on Senate Joint Resolution 63, an identical measure, are attached.

[H. Rept. No. 340, 85th Cong., 1st sess.]

The Committee on Agriculture, to whom was referred the joint resolution (H. J. Res. 172) relating to the stockpile of extra long staple cotton under the Strategic and Critical Materials Stockpiling Act, having considered the same, report favorably thereon without amendment and recommend that the joint resolution do pass.

PURPOSE OF BILL

The purpose of this bill is to require the release from the strategic and critical materials stockpile of 50,000 bales of domestic extra long staple cotton and the sale of such cotton into regular commercial channels by the Commodity Credit Corporation. Under the provisions of the Agricultural Act of 1949 referred to in the resolution, the minimum price at which CCC could sell this cotton would be 105 percent of the current support price plus carrying charges. Actually, the cotton would probably sell somewhat above this price.

Extra long staple cotton is a relatively new crop in the United

States and although production has increased substantially in the past few years, domestic production still falls short of domestic consumption. The growers of this type of cotton have staged an aggressive merchandising campaign and have developed a substantial market for their commodity in this country. As part of this merchandising campaign, they have sought to keep the price of extra long staple cotton at levels low enough to compete successfully with foreign-produced extra long staple cotton and with other fibers. In this connection, the committee has recently reported a bill (H. R. 3654) which will prevent the support level on extra long staple cotton from going up, as it very likely would otherwise do, under the flexible pricing provisions of the Agricultural Act of 1949.

Substantial quantities of this cotton have been placed in the critical materials stockpile. It has been known for some time that the quantity in the stockpile exceeded the stockpile goal and only recently the Office of Defense Mobilization has made a determination that this type of cotton is no longer a critical material. At the same time supplies of this cotton in the United States have become quite short and the producers are fearful that the tight supply situation, combined with price increases which inevitably occur under such supply situations, will cause some of those now using this cotton to turn to other fibers and deprive the long staple cotton producers of part of the market they have succeeded in building up.

For this reason, the producers consider it urgent that the amount of cotton covered by this resolution be released from the stockpile immediately so that it can be made available to the trade in the period between now and the harvest next fall of this year's cotton crop. Particularly in view of the recent action of ODM, there appears to the committee to be no reason why this should not be done.

DEPARTMENTAL VIEWS

The following letter from the Department of Agriculture sets out in more detail reasons for enactment of this legislation at this time.

DEPARTMENT OF AGRICULTURE,
Washington, D. C., April 9, 1957.

Hon. HAROLD D. COOLEY,
Chairman, Committee on Agriculture,
House of Representatives.

DEAR CONGRESSMAN COOLEY: This is in reply to your request of March 13, 1957, for a report on House Joint Resolution 172, a joint resolution relating to the stockpile of extra long staple cotton under the Strategic and Critical Materials Stockpiling Act.

From the standpoint of the responsibilities of this Department, enactment of the proposed legislation would be beneficial. However, we are not in a position to comment on the foreign policy implications of the proposal.

This joint resolution provides that notwithstanding any provision of law, 50,000 bales of domestically grown extra long staple cotton in the stockpile (including any cotton which does not meet current stockpile specifications, established pursuant to the Strategic and Critical Materials Stockpiling Act, as amended) shall be withdrawn and transferred to the Commodity Credit Corporation for sale at not less than the prices at which the Commodity Credit Corporation

10 prices at which the Commodity Credit Corporation may sell

11 its stocks under the minimum pricing provision of section

I

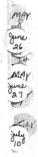

may sell its stocks under the minimum pricing provision of section 407 of the Agricultural Act of 1949, as amended.

Proceeds from such sale, less costs incurred by CCC, including administrative expense, as determined by the Secretary of Agriculture, shall be covered into the Treasury of the United States as miscellaneous receipts.

It is generally agreed by those familiar with the stockpile operations that the current inventory of extra long staple cotton in the stockpile is somewhat larger than is considered necessary to meet the needs for which it was obtained. On this basis, it is our position that at least 50,000 bales can be released from the stockpile, as proposed in the bill, without adversely affecting our supply situation. Since the quantity of extra long staple cotton in the stockpile is classified information, representatives of this Department will be available to meet with the Committee on Agriculture for any further discussion of the matter which may be considered necessary.

The cotton in the stockpile was acquired at prices averaging about $1.05 a pound. The price at which this cotton could now be sold under the provisions of the bill is approximately 63 cents a pound.

The loss to the Government on 50,000 bales, if it were now withdrawn and sold, would be about $10,500,000. Storage on such cotton is costly to the Government, however, and if the quantity specified is not presently needed, it would be better to dispose of it and take the loss in order to avoid further storage expense.

Your attention is invited to the fact that on March 13, 1957, Mr. Arthur S. Flemming, Director, Office of Defense Mobilization, notified Mr. Franklin G. Floete, Administrator, General Services Administration, that his Office had determined, pursuant to section 2 (a) of the Strategic and Critical Materials Stockpiling Act, that (1) extra long staple cotton should be removed from the current list of strategic and critical materials for stockpiling and (2) the stockpile inventory of extra long staple cotton should be sold in accordance with section 3 (e) of the act. We do not believe this action should interfere with enactment by the Congress of House Joint Resolution 172. The stockpile of extra long staple cotton contains substantially more than 50,000 bales; however, even if the executive and legislative branches have no differences of opinion on the plans formulated for selling the entire stockpile of cotton and they can be developed without delay, it will be near the end of the year before any of the cotton could be made available for sale because section 3 (e) of the act requires the disposal plan to be published in the Federal Register and filed with the Congress for 6 months prior to the beginning of execution of the plan. The 50,000 bales covered by the bill are needed to meet demand that exists now and most likely will continue until the new domestic crop is harvested beginning in October.

The Bureau of the Budget advises that there is no objection to the submission of this report.

Sincerely yours,

MARVIN L. McLAIN,
Assistant Secretary.

DEPARTMENT OF STATE,
Washington, April 30, 1957.

DEAR SENATOR ELLENDER: The Department believes that the Committee on Agriculture should know the Department's position on Senate Joint Resolution 63, and therefore transmits herewith its comments on the proposed legislation.

This bill would transfer 50,000 bales of domestically grown extra long staple cotton from the national stockpile to the Commodity Credit Corporation for sale. This Department believes that the legislation in question is not only unnecessary but, if enacted, could be harmful to the national interest of the United States.

The General Services Administration announced on March 18, 1957, that it had been authorized by the Office of Defense Mobilization to draw up a plan for the disposal of the long staple cotton now being held in the national stockpile. Such a plan, according to the GSA announcement, will be submitted to Congress for approval in accordance with the provisions of section 3 (e) of the Strategic and Critical Materials Stock Piling Act of 1946. The GSA has already begun its work on a disposal plan with the intention of submitting it to Congress before the close of the present session.

The Strategic and Critical Materials Stock Piling Act of 1946 contains certain safeguards with regard to disposal which are not to be found in Senate Joint Resolution 63. Section 3 (e) of the 1946 act requires that there be 6 months' notice between the time a plan for disposal has been drawn up, published in the Federal Register, and transmitted to Congress, and the actual commencement of disposal sales. The same section of the act also states that "the plan and date of disposition shall be fixed with due regard to the protection of the United States against avoidable loss on the sale or transfer of the material to be released and the protection of producers, processors, and consumers against avoidable disruption of their usual markets."

The reaction to the GSA announcement of March 18 by governments of countries which grow extra long staple cotton has already been adverse. Egypt and particularly Peru have expressed serious concern lest the disposal of the stockpile of extra long staple cotton affect their economies by competing with their current and future production. This Department has assured these countries, on the basis of the language of the Strategic and Critical Materials Stock Piling Act, that there will be 6 months' notice before disposal and that any disposal will be conducted in an orderly way and over an extended period of time so as to avoid disruption of their markets.

The enactment of Senate Joint Resolution 63, however, without such safeguards could well mean disruption of the markets of Egypt, Peru, and the Sudan. Fifty thousand bales of extra long staple cotton is equivalent to 45 percent of United States consumption of 110,000 bales of this type of cotton during the present cotton marketing year as estimated by the Department of Agriculture. It is equivalent to 53 percent of the import quota of 95,000 bales of extra long staple cotton which has been in effect since 1939 and which became even more restrictive as a result of the enactment of section 202 (a) of the Agricultural Act of 1956.

The disruption of the markets of Egypt, Peru, and the Sudan resulting from the enactment of Senate Joint Resolution 63 could have unfortunate effects on the relations of the United States with

10   prices at which the Commodity Credit Corporation may sell

11   its stocks under the minimum pricing provision of section

these countries. It would represent a serious impediment to a solution of the Middle East problem at this time. It would further alienate these three countries which have been constantly critical of the United States for its cotton policies in recent years.

Furthermore, the enactment of Senate Joint Resolution 63 might adversely affect the stockpiling activities of the United States in other fields. There are a number of commodities that the United States is actively buying for the stockpile, the procurement of which is dependent upon the good will and cooperation of other countries. To these countries the 6-month notice provision of the Strategic and Critical Materials Stock Piling Act is an important safeguard in case of future disposal by the United States. The enactment of Senate Joint Resolution 63, however, would indicate to them that the United States is willing to depart from this important safeguard whenever domestic pressures build up. They would consider that the stockpile is not to be used only for national defense purposes as provided in the 1946 act but instead also for market stability as envisaged by the supporters of Senate Joint Resolution 63. The willingness of these countries to make critical materials available to the United States under such circumstances may be open to question.

For the foregoing reasons, therefore, the Department of State strongly recommends against enactment of Senate Joint Resolution 63. It is hoped that the Congress would permit the disposal planning now underway by GSA to operate instead.

The Bureau of the Budget advises that there is no objection to the submission of this report.

Sincerely yours,

ROBERT C. HILL,
Assistant Secretary.

EXECUTIVE OFFICE OF THE PRESIDENT,
OFFICE OF DEFENSE MOBILIZATION,
Washington, D. C., April 23, 1957.

Hon. ALLEN J. ELLENDER,
Chairman, Committee on Agriculture and Forestry,
United States Senate, Washington, D. C.

DEAR SENATOR ELLENDER: This has further reference to your request for our comments on Senate Joint Resolution 63, a joint resolution relating to the stockpile of extra staple cotton under the Strategic and Critical Materials Stockpiling Act.

The Office of Defense Mobilization, in carrying out its responsibilities for the administration of the national stockpile recently concluded that long staple cotton should be removed from the strategic and critical materials list for stockpiling and that present inventories of long staple cotton should be sold.

Section 3 (e) of the Strategic and Critical Materials Stock Piling Act stipulates that no disposition shall be made until 6 months after publication of notice in the Federal Register and that in these circumstances the plan of disposition must be approved by Congress. Congressional approval could be indicated by a concurrent resolution.

The apparent purpose of Senate Joint Resolution 63 is to waive the 6-month waiting period with regard to the sale of 50,000 bales of the stockpile inventory of extra-long-staple cotton.

through June 30, 1958, for emergency conservation measures (p. 8547) and $11,500,000 (instead of $15,000,000 as proposed by the Senate) for emergency feed and seed assistance (p. 8548). Rejected, 105 to 218, a motion by Rep. Boland to agree to the Senate amendment providing $14,000,000 for a Federal flood insurance program (pp. 8548-60). This bill now goes to the Senate for consideration. (For other items of interest see Digest 88.)

Extra-long-staple cotton first became a substantial domestic crop as a result of Government-financial incentives which were provided to encourage the development of domestic production to meet the heavy demands for this material during the Korean period. As a result of this program, cotton growers have gradually increased the size of their crops during the past several years to such an extent as to eliminate our reliance on foreign sources of supply during times of national emergency. This factor was the basis of the Office of Defense Mobilization's determination that extra-long-staple cotton should be removed from the list of materials for stockpiling.

We have been advised that the proposed legislation is sponsored by the growers of extra-long-staple cotton for several reasons, among which are:

Egypt's decision to sell a substantial portion of its crop to Communist Russia has resulted in a shortage of this material for domestic purposes. Since the current domestic crop will not be available before October of this year, it is feared that current consumers of this type of cotton will switch to synthetics if there is any substantial rise in price or if the current shortage continues. In order to preclude this possibility, it is urged that current needs of domestic consumers should be satisfied by the immediate sale of 50,000 bales from stockpile inventory without regard to the statutory formalities. Proponents of the measure point out further that such action would help to stabilize this important segment of our mobilization base.

On the other hand, the legislative and administrative history of the Stockpile Act clearly indicates that the time limitation on disposition was placed in the Strategic and Critical Materials Stock Piling Act in order to assure friendly foreign countries that the United States had no intention of using stockpile inventories to influence world market conditions. We have been informed that any modification or exception to this rule would establish a bad precedent and compromise the integrity of the stockpile concept.

It is our opinion that the financial and security advantages which could accrue to the United States from the sale of 50,000 bales of extra long staple cotton in the manner proposed by Senate Joint Resolution 63 are outweighed by the long-range advantage of maintaining free world confidence in the stockpile operation.

Accordingly, we do not recommend enactment of Senate Joint Resolution 63 in its present form.

The Bureau of the Budget advises that it has no objection to the submission of this report.

Sincerely yours,

GORDON GRAY, *Director.*

10 prices at which the Commodity Credit Corporation may sell

11 its stocks under the minimum pricing provision of section

5. HOUSING. The
   4602, to enco
   464). p. 844

6. ELECTRIFICATIO
   Senate's unfi
       Sen. Hum
   the Carlton C
   Sen. Hum
   resolution ur;
   increased. p

7. FLOOD INSURANCI
   Federal Flood

8. STUDENT EXCHAN(
   value of the :

9. PERSONNEL. Se
   reported to tl
   Neuberger's s

10. FISCAL POLICY.
    Carlson, Laus
    fiscal and mo:
    inserted Trea:
    Committee on t

11. WATER RESOURCE:
    the recent flo
    value of floo

12. FOOD DISTRIBUTI
    steps to stock

13. IMPORTS. Rece
    import of dri

14. LANDS. Receive
    near Parker D

15. WHEAT. Sen. Ca
    urging a /yes'
    20. p./8443

16. APPROPRIATIONS.
    plemental appr
    million (inste
    through June 30, 1958, for emergency conservation measures (p. 854;
    $11,500,000 (instead of $15,000,000 as proposed by the Senate) for
    feed and seed assistance (p. 8548). Rejected, 156 to 218, a motio:
    Boland to agree to the Senate amendment providing $14,000,000 for
    flood insurance program (pp. 8548-60). This bill now goes to the S
    consideration. (For other items of interest see Digest 88.)

Calendar No. 470

85TH CONGRESS
1ST SESSION
H. J. RES. 172

[Report No. 463]

IN THE SENATE OF THE UNITED STATES

MAY 8, 1957

Read twice and referred to the Committee on Agriculture and Forestry

JUNE 18, 1957

Reported by Mr. EASTLAND, without amendment

JOINT RESOLUTION

Relating to the stockpile of extra long staple cotton under the
Strategic and Critical Materials Stockpiling Act.

1   *Resolved by the Senate and House of Representatives*

2   *of the United States of America in Congress assembled,*

3   That notwithstanding any other provision of law, fifty thou-

4   sand bales of domestically grown extra long staple cotton in

5   the stockpile (including any cotton which does not meet cur-

6   rent stockpile specifications) established pursuant to the

7   Strategic and Critical Materials Stockpiling Act, as amended

8   (50 U. S. C. 98), shall be withdrawn and transferred to the

9   Commodity Credit Corporation for sale at not less than the

10   prices at which the Commodity Credit Corporation may sell

11   its stocks under the minimum pricing provision of section

2

1   407 of the Agricultural Act of 1949, as amended. Proceeds

2   from such sale, less costs incurred by Commodity Credit Cor-

3   poration, including administrative expense, as determined

4   by the Secretary of Agriculture, shall be covered into the

5   Treasury of the United States as miscellaneous receipts.

      Passed the House of Representatives May 6, 1957.

      Attest: RALPH R. ROBERTS,

                                  Clerk.

Calendar No. 470

80TH CONGRESS
1ST SESSION

H. J. RES. 172

[Report No. 463]

JOINT RESOLUTION

Relating to the stockpile of extra long staple
cotton under the Strategic and Critical
Materials Stockpiling Act.

MAY 8, 1957

Read twice and referred to the Committee on
Agriculture and Forestry

JUNE 18, 1957

Reported without amendment

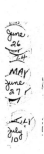

Sen. Goldwater criticized the Federal grant-in-aid programs and inserted a table showing the new grants proposed for 1958. pp. 9238-9

29. INTEREST RATES. Sen. Bush inserted an editorial from the Wall Street Journal urging greater consideration for people who save. pp. 9244-5

30. WHEAT. Sen. Humphrey inserted correspondence with the Farmers' Union Wheat Referendum Committee, in which he called the wheat vote "a vote of repudiation and censure for the Secretary of Agriculture." p. 9257

31. EDUCATIONAL EXCHANGE. Sen. Fulbright inserted articles attacking certain allegations that Fulbright scholars were spies. pp. 9258-9

18. PERSONNEL. At the request of Sen. Purtell, passed over S. 25, to make the dates of increase of compensation for wage board employees retroactive to 30 days after submission of their petition. p. 9260

19. SAFETY. At the request of Sen. Purtell, passed over S. 931, to create a Federal Safety Division in the Department of Labor. p. 9260

20. COTTON. At the request of Sen. Purtell, passed over H.J. Res. 172, to release 50,000 bales of extra long staple cotton from the Strategic and Critical Materials Stockpile. p. 9269

21. HOUSING. At the request of Sen. Talmadge, passed over H.R. 4602, to encourage new veterans' housing in rural areas. p. 9269

22. FOREIGN AFFAIRS. The Foreign Relations Committee reported without amendment S. 603, to require that international agreements other than treaties be transmitted to the Senate 60 days after their execution (S. Rept. 521)(p. 9217). At the request of Sen. Purtell, passed over this bill (pp. 9260-1).

23. ST. LAWRENCE SEAWAY. Passed as reported S. 1174, to increase the borrowing authority of the St. Lawrence Seaway Corporation (pp. 9260, 9289-90). The bill had been reported with amendment earlier in the day by the Foreign Relations Committee (S. Rept. 525) (p. 9217).

24. PURCHASING. Sen. Sparkman criticized the procurement practices of the Defense Department, and inserted a tabulation of common-use items which are procured by negotiation. pp. 9313-21

25. APPROPRIATIONS. The Appropriations Committee reported with amendments H.R. 7599, the legislative appropriation bill for 1958 (S. Rept. 533). p. 9222

26. TRANSPORTATION. The Interstate and Foreign Commerce Committee reported without amendment S. 1461, to authorize revocation of ICC licensees for non-willful (as well as willful) offenses (S. Rept. 531). p. 9222

27. ELECTRIFICATION; RECLAMATION. Sen. Morse inserted an editorial, "Wasters on the Run," which cheered the passage of the Hells Canyon dam bill. pp. 9248-9
    Sen. Humphrey inserted a Virginia, Minn., electric cooperative's resolution opposing any increase in REA loan rates. pp. 9220-1

28. FEDERAL AID. Sen. Smith, N.J., inserted the President's address to the Conference of State Governor's in which he urged establishment of a task force to study Federal-State tax bases. pp. 9236-8
    Sen. Goldwater criticized the Federal grant-in-aid programs and inserted a table showing the new grants proposed for 1958. pp. 9238-9

29. INTEREST RATES. Sen. Bush inserted an editorial from the Wall Street Journal urging greater consideration for people who save. pp. 9244-5

30. WHEAT. Sen. Humphrey inserted correspondence with the Farmers' Union Wheat Referendum Committee, in which he called the wheat vote "a vote of repudiation and censure for the Secretary of Agriculture." p. 9257

31. EDUCATIONAL EXCHANGE. Sen. Fulbright inserted articles attacking certain allegations that Fulbright scholars were spies. pp. 9258-9

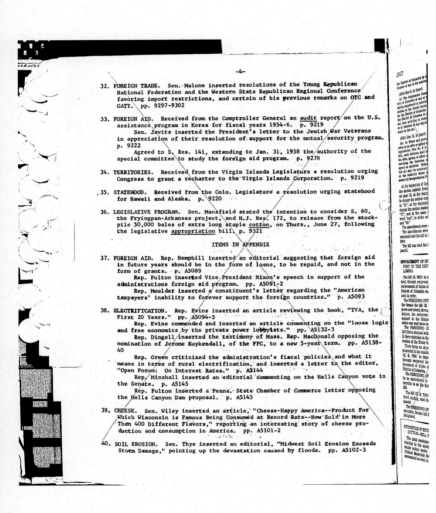

-4-

32. FOREIGN TRADE. Sen. Malone inserted resolutions of the Young Republican National Federation and the Western State Republican Regional Conference favoring import restrictions, and certain of his previous remarks on OTC and GATT. pp. 9297-9302

33. FOREIGN AID. Received from the Comptroller General an audit report on the U.S. assistance program in Korea for fiscal years 1954-6. p. 9219
    Sen. Javits inserted the President's letter to the Jewish War Veterans in appreciation of their resolution of support for the mutual security program. p. 9222
    Agreed to S. Res. 141, extending to Jan. 31, 1958 the authority of the special committee to study the foreign aid program. p. 9278

34. TERRITORIES. Received from the Virgin Islands Legislature a resolution urging Congress to grant a recharter to the Virgin Islands Corporation. p. 9219

35. STATEHOOD. Received from the Colo. Legislature a resolution urging statehood for Hawaii and Alaska. p. 9220

36. LEGISLATIVE PROGRAM. Sen. Mansfield stated the intention to consider S. 60, the Fryingpan-Arkansas project, and H.J. Res. 172, to release from the stockpile 50,000 bales of extra long staple cotton, on Thurs., June 27, following the legislative appropriation bill. p. 9321

ITEMS IN APPENDIX

37. FOREIGN AID. Rep. Hemphill inserted an editorial suggesting that foreign aid in future years should be in the form of loans, to be repaid, and not in the form of grants. p. A5089
    Rep. Fulton inserted Vice President Nixon's speech in support of the administrations foreign aid program. pp. A5091-2
    Rep. Moulder inserted a constituent's letter regarding the "American taxpayers' inability to forever support the foreign countries." p. A5093

38. ELECTRIFICATION. Rep. Evins inserted an article reviewing the book, "TVA, the First 20 Years." pp. A5094-5
    Rep. Evins commended and inserted an article commenting on the "loose logic and free economics by the private power lobbyists." pp. A5132-3
    Rep. Dingell inserted the testimony of Mass. Rep. MacDonald opposing the nomination of Jerome Kuykendall, of the FPC, to a new 5-year term. pp. A5138-40
    Rep. Green criticized the administration's fiscal policies and what it means in terms of rural electrification, and inserted a letter to the editor, "Open Forum: On Interest Rates." p. A5144
    Rep. Minshall inserted an editorial commenting on the Hells Canyon vote in the Senate. p. A5145
    Rep. Fulton inserted a Penna. State Chamber of Commerce letter opposing the Hells Canyon Dam proposal. p. A5145

39. CHEESE. Sen. Wiley inserted an article, "Cheese-Happy America--Product For Which Wisconsin is Famous Being Consumed at Record Rate--Now Sold in More Than 400 Different Flavors," reporting an interesting story of cheese production and consumption in America. pp. A5101-2

40. SOIL EROSION. Sen. Thye inserted an editorial, "Midwest Soil Erosion Exceeds Storm Damage," pointing up the devastation caused by floods. pp. A5102-3

the District of Columbia by the Corporation Counsel or any of his assistants.

After line 9, to insert:

(c) The Corporation Counsel of the District of Columbia or any of his assistants is, hereby empowered to maintain an action or actions in the United States District Court for the District of Columbia in the name of the District of Columbia to enjoin any person from soliciting in violation of this act or in violation of any regulation made pursuant to this act.

After line 16, to insert:

SEC. 14. Where any provision of this act refers to an office or agency abolished by Reorganization Plan No. 5 of 1952 (66 Stat. 824), such reference shall be deemed to be the office, agency, or officer now or hereafter exercising the functions of the office or agency so abolished. Nothing contained in this act shall be construed as a limitation on the authority vested in the Commissioners by Reorganization Plan No. 5 of 1952.

At the beginning of line 25, to change the section number from "13" to "15"; on page 13, at the beginning of line 5, to change the section number from "14" to "16"; at the beginning of line 7, to change the section number from "15" to "17", and in the same line, after the word "and", to strike out "14" and insert "16."

The amendments were agreed to.

The amendments were ordered to be engrossed and the bill to be read a third time.

The bill was read the third time, and passed.

ENFORCEMENT OF DUTIES OF SUPPORT IN THE DISTRICT OF COLUMBIA

The bill (S. 2032) to improve and extend, through reciprocal legislation, the enforcement of duties of support in the District of Columbia was announced as next in order.

The PRESIDING OFFICER laid before the Senate the bill (H. R. 7249) to improve and extend, through reciprocal legislation, the enforcement of duties of support in the District of Columbia, which was read twice by its title.

The PRESIDING OFFICER. House bill 7249 is identical with Senate bill 2032. Is there objection to the present consideration of the House bill?

There being no objection, the Senate proceeded to the consideration of the bill (H. R. 7249) to improve and extend, through reciprocal legislation, the enforcement of duties of support in the District of Columbia.

The PRESIDING OFFICER. If there be no amendment to be proposed, the question is on the third reading of the bill.

The bill (H. R. 7249) was ordered to a third reading, read the third time, and passed.

The PRESIDING OFFICER. Without objection, Senate bill 2032 is indefinitely postponed.

STOCKPILE OF EXTRA LONG STAPLE COTTON—BILL PASSED OVER

The joint resolution (H. J. Res. 172) relating to the stockpile of extra long staple cotton under the Strategic and Critical Materials Stockpiling Act, was announced as next in order.

Mr. PURTELL. Mr. President, in the opinion of the calendar committee, this is not proper consent calendar business, and I ask that the bill go over.

Mr. MANSFIELD. Mr. President, will the Senator withhold his objection?

Mr. PURTELL. I withhold my objection.

Mr. MANSFIELD. Is it the contention of the Senator from Connecticut that the joint resolution ought to be called up later, and not discussed on a call of the calendar?

Mr. PURTELL. I have no objection to its being called up, and will not object to doing so, but there is about $10 million involved, and I do not feel it is proper calendar business.

The PRESIDING OFFICER. The bill will be passed over.

BILLS PASSED OVER

The bill (H. R. 4602) to encourage new residential construction for veterans' housing in rural areas by raising the maximum amount in which direct loans may be made, and for other purposes, was announced as next in order.

Mr. TALMADGE. Over.

The PRESIDING OFFICER. The bill will be passed over.

The bill (S. 1459) to amend section 208 (c) of the Interstate Commerce Act, as amended, was announced as next in order.

Mr. TALMADGE. Over.

The PRESIDING OFFICER. The bill will be passed over.

LEASE OF UNASSIGNED LANDS ON THE COLORADO RIVER INDIAN RESERVATION

The bill (S. 2161) to amend the act of August 14, 1955 (69 Stat. 725), was considered, ordered to be engrossed for a third reading, read the third time, and passed, as follows:

Be it enacted, etc., That the act of August 14, 1955 (69 Stat. 725), is amended by deleting the words "2 years" wherever they appear and by inserting in lieu thereof "4 years."

Mr. GOLDWATER. Mr. President, I ask unanimous consent that a statement I have prepared in connection with the passage of S. 2161 be printed in the RECORD at this point.

There being no objection, the statement was ordered to be printed in the RECORD, as follows:

STATEMENT BY SENATOR GOLDWATER CONCERNING PRESENT AND PROPOSED CONSTRUCTION OF THE COLORADO RIVER, INDIAN IRRIGATION PROJECT

The Colorado River Indian irrigation project is located about 100 miles north of Yuma on the Arizona side of the Colorado River. The average project elevation is 325 mean sea level. The climate is arid, averaging only 5 inches of precipitation a year. Temperatures range from 122° maximum to 16° minimum. The ultimate project area consists of approximately 100,000 acres of fertile river bottom lands which are extremely productive when provided with an adequate water supply.

The project was authorized by the act of March 3, 1867 (14 Stat. 514), by an appropriation of $50,000, a portion of which was for the purpose of constructing a canal to irrigate the reservation. Work was started in 1867 on the construction of a canal and

a headgate near the present Indian agency. In 1871 the canal was extended some 3 miles up the river to a heading at the site of the present diversion dam. Floods in the Colorado River made it difficult to maintain the canal although it was used from time to time until 1898 when a steam-driven centrifugal pump was installed near the head of the irrigable area and the upper portion of the canal and headworks were abandoned. The original pumping plant was renewed and enlarged in 1929 to provide capacity to irrigate some 6,000 acres.

The pumping plant was considered as a temporary measure pending development of additional land on the reservation. The construction of Headgate Rock diversion dam across the Colorado River was authorized by section 2 of the River and Harbor Act of August 30, 1935 (49 Stat. 1039). The dam, a reinforced concrete structure, appurtenant works and a section of the main canal were completed under contract in 1942 at an estimated cost of approximately $4,580,000. The main canal and distribution system was designed and is being constructed with sufficient capacity to irrigate 100,000 acres each year with a diversion duty of 6 acre-feet per acre.

With the completion of Headgate Rock diversion dam and the first section of main canal, it was possible to discontinue operation of the pumping plant in favor of a gravity system. The main canal and several of the laterals were immediately extended to the south to provide service to the Poston war relocation camps located some 15 miles south of the Indian agency.

In 1946 a large scale program of land preparation was initiated on the project in connection with the program to relocate other Indians of the Colorado River Basin on irrigated reservation farms. Since that time approximately 24,000 acres of new lands have been cleared and subjugated and irrigation facilities have been provided to serve the area. The present project works include the Diversion Dam; 19½ miles of main canal with 13 reinforced concrete structures; 267 miles of laterals including 2,770 concrete control structures; 124 miles of drains; 7 miles of levees; and 5 wells and electric-pumping plants used for both drainage and irrigation. An area of 37,000 acres is now provided with irrigation facilities.

The purchase and sale of power was authorized by the act of June 18, 1940 (54 Stat. 422), the Indian reservation having been given a preferential right to the purchase of power from the generating plant of the Bureau of Reclamation at Parker Dam. All power is purchased from the Parker Dam plant and none is generated on the Colorado River project. The system consists of 70 miles of 34.5 kilovolt transmission line and distribution systems to serve some 425 customers on both the Arizona and California sides of the river on and in the vicinity of the Indian reservation.

Total construction costs as of May 31, 1957, for the irrigation and power facilities are $18,114,000.

In order to subjugate the lands and complete the balance of 65,000 acres of the project, a large amount of construction work remains to be done. This work is estimated to cost a total of $26,489,460 at 1956 price levels.

The details are as follows:

Diversion dam alteration	$4,960
Main canal lining	660,000
Lateral system—230 miles	5,525,000
Drainage	1,619,000
Bridges, farm access	404,000
Flood control	180,500
Road grading and bridges	2,506,000
Land subjugation	12,890,000
Farm ditches	2,700,000
Total	26,489,460

The project area, when fully developed, will provide farms for some 1,250 Indian families. The development of such an area for irrigated farming will accelerate the growth of Parker, Valley Center, and other towns in the race which should provide employment opportunities for both Indians and non-Indians.

REPEAL OF SECTION 1157 OF TITLE 18 OF THE UNITED STATES CODE, AS AMENDED

The bill (H. R. 3836) to repeal section 1157 of title 18 of the United States Code, as amended, was considered, ordered to a third reading, read the third time, and passed.

EDUCATIONAL LEAVE OF EMPLOYEES OF THE BUREAU OF INDIAN AFFAIRS

The bill (H. R. 3837) to amend the act of August 24, 1912, as amended, with reference to educational leave of employees of the Bureau of Indian Affairs was considered, ordered to a third reading, read the third time, and passed.

RECOUPMENT OF FUNDS EXPENDED IN COOPERATION WITH THE SCHOOL BOARD OF KLAMATH COUNTY, OREG.

The bill (S. 1894) to amend the law with respect to the recoupment of funds expended in cooperation with the school board of Klamath County, Oreg., because of the attendance of Indian children, and for other purposes, was announced as next in order.

The PRESIDING OFFICER. The Chair lays before the Senate a bill coming over from the House of Representatives, which is an identical bill.

The bill (H. R. 7050) to amend the law with respect to the recoupment of funds expended in cooperation with the school board of Klamath County, Oreg., because of the attendance of Indian children, and for other purposes; was read twice by its title.

Mr. NEUBERGER. Mr. President, S. 1894 and H. R. 7050, which has been passed by the House, are identical bills. The purpose of the proposed legislation is to amend the Klamath Termination Act of the 83d Congress with respect to the recoupment of funds expended in cooperation with the school board of Klamath County, Oreg., because of the attendance of Indian schoolchildren.

Under section 24 of the Klamath Termination Act, the obligation of Klamath County would have been repealed following the final termination date. However, the Governor of Oregon has elected for the State to come under section 10 of Public Law 874, 81st Congress, beginning July 1, 1957. Therefore, unless the recoupment obligation is repealed, the county will continue to be subject to the recoupment provisions, but will not be eligible for Johnson-O'Malley contract funds with which to make payments.

The enactment of this legislation will place Klamath County in the same position as other school district whose obligations have been canceled under statutes enacted in the 84th and prior Congresses. The bill is fair and justified, and I ask that the bill be considered.

The PRESIDING OFFICER. Is there objection to the present consideration of the bill?

There being no objection, the Senate proceeded to consider the bill.

The PRESIDING OFFICER. The question is on the third reading of the bill.

The bill (H. R. 7050) was ordered to a third reading, read the third time, and passed.

The PRESIDING OFFICER. Without objection, Senate bill 1894 is indefinitely postponed.

TRANSFER OF COYOTE VALLEY INDIAN RANCHERIA

The bill (H. R. 6692) to authorize the transfer of the Coyote Valley Indian Rancheria to the Secretary of the Army, and for other purposes, was considered, ordered to a third reading, read the third time, and passed.

ESTABLISHMENT OF NATIONAL OUTDOOR RECREATION RESOURCES REVIEW COMMISSION

The bill (S. 846) for the establishment of a National Outdoor Recreation Resources Review Commission to study the public lands and other land and water areas of the United States, and for other purposes, was announced as next in order.

Mr. PURTELL. Over, by request.

Mr. ANDERSON. Mr. President, I wonder if my friend from Connecticut will withhold his objection.

Mr. PURTELL. I am very happy to do so.

Mr. ANDERSON. I recognize that it is entirely proper to object to a bill of this nature on the call of the calendar, but I wish to make a brief statement.

Nearly all the wildlife and conservation organizations with which I am acquainted have been working steadily on this matter for some years. The chairman of the Interior and Insular Affairs Committee, the Senator from Montana [Mr. MURRAY], the Senator from Colorado [Mr. CARROLL], the Senator from Oregon [Mr. NEUBERGER], and I, from the Democratic side, have joined in sponsoring the bill, along with the Senator from Utah [Mr. WATKINS], the Senator from Wyoming [Mr. BARRETT], the Senator from California [Mr. KUCHEL], the Senator from Colorado [Mr. ALLOTT], and the Senator from Arizona [Mr. GOLDWATER], from the Republican side. There is nothing political about this measure.

As the number of people who visit our national parks increases, there is involved a very definite problem of properly accommodating them, for example. Yellowstone Park, which belong to all the people of the country, and not merely to rich people. Priorities are needed in order to get inside the park. The number of people visiting the western lands and parks of America is increasing tremendously. It would be the sheerest kind of rolly to rail to pass the bill which provides only for a survey to determine what is needed in order to accommodate persons who will visit our parks in increasing numbers.

Mr. PURTELL. Mr. President, I had objected by request. The Senator who objected now tells me that he is withdrawing his objection. I therefore have no objection to the bill.

The PRESIDING OFFICER. Is there objection to the consideration of the bill?

There being no objection, the Senate proceeded to consider the bill (S. 846) for the establishment of a National Outdoor Recreation Resources Review Commission to study the public lands and other land and water areas of the United States, and for other purposes, which had been reported from the Committee on Interior and Insular Affairs with amendments on page 1, line 3, after the word "to", to strike out "preserve and develop for the" and insert "preserve, develop, and assure accessability to all"; on page 4, line 22, after the word "request", to strike out "each Federal agency" and insert "the Secretary of each Federal Department or head of any independent agency which includes an agency or agencies"; on page 5, line 2, after the word "and", to insert "he shall appoint for"; in line 3, after the word "agency", to strike out "shall appoint,"; in line 21, after the word "all", to insert "agencies and groups whose assistance in accomplishing the purposes of this act will be required in arriving at sound methods and"; on page 7, line 14, after the word "Congress", to insert "and shall cease to exist not later than one year thereafter"; in line 19, after the word "Commission", to insert "on its own initiative or"; on page 8, line 1, after the word "States", to insert "and to transfer necessary funds to Federal agencies"; in line 4, after the word "States", to insert "or Federal agencies", and on page 9, line 2, after the word "expended", to strike out "but not later than June 30, 1960"; so as to make the bill read:

Be it enacted, etc., That in order to preserve, develop, and assure accessibility to all American people of present and future generations such quality and quantity of outdoor recreation resources as will be necessary and desirable for individual enjoyment, and to assure the spiritual, cultural, and physical benefits that such outdoor recreation provides; in order to inventory and evaluate the outdoor recreation resources and opportunities of the Nation, to determine the types and location of such resources and opportunities which will be required by present and future generations; and in order to make comprehensive information and recommendations leading to these goals available to the President, the Congress, and the individual States and Territories, there is hereby authorized and created a bipartisan Outdoor Recreation Resources Review Commission.

SEC. 2. For the purposes of this act—

(1) "Commission" shall mean the Outdoor Recreation Resources Review Commission;

(2) "Outdoor recreation resources" shall mean the land and water areas and the products of such areas of the United States, its Territories and possessions which provide opportunities for outdoor recreation, including but not limited to such pursuits as

long staple cotton from the Strategic Materials stockpile. This measure will
now be sent to the President. pp. 9398-9

3. BUILDINGS. The Public Works Committee reported without amendment S. 2261, to
amend the Federal lease-purchase program relative to the distribution and
approval of new public buildings projects (S. Rept. 540). p. 9358

4. TRANSPORTATION. The Interstate and Foreign Commerce Committee reported with
amendments S. 1383, to require the certification by the ICC of freight forwarders
(S. Rept. 542). p. 9358
        Passed without amendment S. 1459, to require truck and bus charter
operators to apply for ICC approval. pp. 9435-6

attendance of Indian schoolchildren.

Under section 24 of the Klamath Termination Act, the obligation of Klamath County would have been repealed following the final termination date. However, the Governor of Oregon has elected for the State to come under section 10 of Public Law 874, 81st Congress, beginning July 1, 1957. Therefore, unless the recoupment obligation is repealed, the county will continue to be subject to the recoupment provisions, but will not be eligible for Johnson-O'Malley contract funds with which to make payments.

The enactment of this legislation will place Klamath County in the same position as other school district whose obligations have been canceled under stat-

Wyoming [Mr. Barrett], the Senator from California [Mr. Kuchel], the Senator from Colorado [Mr. Allott], and the Senator from Arizona [Mr. Goldwater], from the Republican side. There is nothing political about this measure.

As the number of people who visit our national parks increases, there is involved a very definite problem of properly accommodating them, for example, Yellowstone Park, which belong to all the people of the country, and not merely to rich people. Priorities are needed in order to get inside the park. The number of people visiting the western lands and parks of America is increasing tremendously. It would be the sheerest kind of folly to fail to pass the bill which

mine the types and location of such resources and opportunities which will be required by present and future generations; and in order to make comprehensive information and recommendations leading to these goals available to the President, the Congress, and the individual States and Territories, there is hereby authorized and created a bipartisan Outdoor Recreation Resources Review Commission.

Sec. 2. For the purposes of this act—

(1) "Commission" shall mean the Outdoor Recreation Resources Review Commission;

(2) "Outdoor recreation resources" shall mean the land and water areas and the products of such areas of the United States, its Territories and possessions which provide opportunities for outdoor recreation, including but not limited to such pursuits as

Digest of CONGRESSIONAL PROCEEDINGS

OF INTEREST TO THE DEPARTMENT OF AGRICULTURE

OFFICE OF BUDGET AND FINANCE
(For Department Staff Only)

Issued   June 28, 1957
For actions of   June 27, 1957
85th-1st, No. 112

CONTENTS

HIGHLIGHTS: (See Page 5.)

SENATE

1. FOREIGN TRADE; SURPLUS COMMODITIES. Disagreed with the House amendments to
S. 1314, to extend Public Law 480 until 1958, and appointed as conferees Sens.
Ellender, Johnston, Holland, Eastland, Humphrey, Aiken, Young, Thye, and
Hickenlooper. Consideration of H.R. 6974, a similar bill, was indefinitely
postponed. p. 9382

2. COTTON. Passed without amendment H.J. Res. 172, to release 50,000 bales of extra
long staple cotton from the Strategic Materials stockpile. This measure will
now be sent to the President. pp. 9398-9

3. BUILDINGS. The Public Works Committee reported without amendment S. 2261, to
amend the Federal lease-purchase program relative to the distribution and
approval of new public buildings projects (S. Rept. 540). p. 9358

4. TRANSPORTATION. The Interstate and Foreign Commerce Committee reported with
amendments S. 1383, to require the certification by the ICC of freight forwarders
(S. Rept. 542). p. 9358
    Passed without amendment S. 1459, to require truck and bus charter
operators to apply for ICC approval. pp. 9435-6

5. FOREIGN AFFAIRS. Passed, with an amendment to exempt agreements under the Atomic Energy Act of 1954, S. 603, to require the transmission to the Senate within 60 days of execution, all international agreements . pp. 9436-7
   Sen. Wiley inserted a report on the 1957 Bricker Amendment.
   pp. 9368-74

6. MINERALS. Passed without amendment H.R. 4748, to extend to 1958 the time during which annual assessment work may be done on unpatented mining claims. This bill will now be sent to the President. pp. 9432-3
   Sen. Neuberger criticized the administration of Public Law 359, 84th Congress, which opened to mining claims 7.2 million acres of Federally controlled lands, and inserted a series of articles on the wisdom of opening public lands to mining interests. pp. 9378-80

7. APPROPRIATIONS. Both Houses agreed to the conference report on H.R. 6070, the independent offices appropriation bill for 1958. This bill will now be sent to the President. pp. 9422-4, 9442-6
   Agreed to the conference report on H.R. 6287, the Labor-HEW appropriation bill for 1958. This bill will now be sent to the President. pp. 9382-8
   Passed as reported H.R. 7599, the Legislative branch appropriation bill for 1958. pp. 9404-8

8. ELECTRIFICATION; RECLAMATION. Passed as reported S. 60, to authorize construction of the Fryingpan-Arkansas reclamation project, rejecting two amendments by Sen. Kuchel which would require the Secretary of the Interior to comply with compacts now applying to the river, and stating that the law should not constitute any sort of commitment for further water transfers. pp. 9410, 9416-22, 9424-32

9. RESEARCH. Received from this Department a report on the State agricultural experiment stations for fiscal year 1956. p. 9358

10. FEDERAL AID. Sen. Smith, N.J., inserted two editorials on the President's proposal to study Federal-State relations and the division of functions between them. pp. 9363-4

11. BUDGET. Sen. Goldwater inserted his comments on, and Sen. Bush inserted excerpts from, the report on Fiscal policy implications of the economic outlook and budget developments by the Joint Committee on the Economic Report. pp. 9364-6

12. INTEREST RATES. Sen. Humphrey inserted a series of articles on interest rates and the administration's fiscal policy. pp. 9399-9404

13. WATER RESOURCES. Sen. Morton called the Ohio River Valley "The Ruhr of the U.S." and pointed out the present state of development of its water resources. pp. 9410-12

14. SOIL CONSERVATION. Sen. Yarborough stated that a report of the Soil Conservation Service showed the values of soil conservation in preventing flood damage and protecting the land, and inserted an editorial on the importance of proper care for soil. p. 9424

15. LEGISLATIVE PROGRAM. Sen. Mansfield announced that the conference report on the Interior appropriation bill should be received Mon., July 1, and that the Defense Department appropriation bill should also be considered then. p. 9437

16. ADJOURNED until Mon., July 1. pp. 9437-8

United States on May 1, 1957, and for whom a petition for quota immigrant status under section 203 (a) (1) (A) of the Immigration and Nationality Act (aliens whose services are urgently needed in the United States) had been approved. Similar authority is granted with respect to the spouse and children of any such alien who were in the United States on May 1, 1957, and a nonquota immigrant status is authorized for the spouse and children of any such alien who were not in the United States on such date.

SECTION 5. ALIENS DEPORTABLE OR EXCLUDABLE BECAUSE OF MISREPRESENTATION

Section 5 (which is the same as sec. 4 of H. R. 8123) waives, as a ground of deportation, the procurement of a visa by fraud or misrepresentation (including misrepresentation of nationality). In the case of any alien who is the spouse, parent, or child of a citizen or of an alien lawfully admitted for permanent residence. A similar waiver is provided in the case of any other alien who entered the United States between December 22, 1945, and November 1, 1954, but only if he misrepresented his nationality, birthplace, identity, or residence because of fear of persecution if he were repatriated to his former home or residence, and not to evade the quota restrictions or a personal investigation.

Subsection (b) of such section provides that an alien who is the spouse, parent, or child of a citizen or of an alien lawfully admitted for permanent residence shall not, after the date of enactment of this act, be subject to exclusion on the grounds of procurement of a visa by fraud or misrepresentation, or on the grounds of perjury in connection therewith, if the Attorney General has consented to the alien's applying or reapplying for a visa and for admission to the United States.

SECTION 5. ALIENS EXCLUDABLE BECAUSE OF TUBERCULOSIS

Subsection (a) of section 5 (which is the same as sec. 5 of H. R. 8123) waives the provisions of paragraph (6) of section 212 (a) of the Immigration and Nationality Act, as far as they relate to aliens afflicted with tuberculosis, in the case of an alien who is the spouse, parent, child, or minor unmarried adopted child of a United States citizen, or of an alien lawfully admitted for permanent residence, and who is accompanying or following to join such United States citizen or alien.

Subsection (b) of such section provides that the Attorney General shall report to the Congress in any case in which paragraph (6) of section 212 (a) is waived pursuant to such section.

Subsection (c) of such section provides for the expiration of such section on June 30, 1959.

SECTION 6. GRANTING NONQUOTA STATUS TO CERTAIN ALIENS

Section 6 (which is the same as section 6 of H. R. 8123) provides that any alien eligible for a quota immigrant status under paragraph (3) or (3) of section 203 (a) of the Immigration and Nationality Act (parents of citizens and the spouses and children of aliens lawfully admitted for permanent residence) on the basis of a petition approved by the Attorney General prior to March 2, 1957 shall be issued a nonquota immigrant visa if he is otherwise admissible under such act, and is found to have retained his relationship to the petitioner, as established in the approved petition, at the time he makes application for an immigrant visa and admission to the United States.

SECTION 7. ISSUANCE OF CERTAIN SPECIAL NONQUOTA IMMIGRANT VISAS AUTHORIZED UNDER THE REFUGEE RELIEF ACT OF 1953

Subsection (a) of section 7 provides for issuance to certain refugee-escapees of the special nonquota immigrant visas authorized to be issued under paragraphs (1), (9), (10), and (11) of section 4 (a) of the Refugee Relief Act of 1953, but which remained unissued on January 1, 1957.

Subsection (b) of such section defines refugee-escapee, for purposes of subsection (a), as any alien who, because of persecution or fear of persecution on account of race, religion, or political opinion has fled or shall flee from any Communist, Communist-dominated or Communist-occupied area, or from any country within the general area of the Middle East, and who cannot return to such area, or to such country, on account of race, religion, or political opinion.

Subsection (c) of such section provides that such section shall not be held to extend the Refugee Relief Act of 1953, or to authorize the issuance of special nonquota immigrant visas in excess of the number provided in section 3 of such act.

SECTION 8. TERMINATION OF CERTAIN QUOTA-MORTGAGING REQUIREMENTS

Section 8 (which is similar to section 8 of H. R. 8123) provides that the quota deductions required under the provisions of the Displaced Persons Act of 1948, the act of June 30, 1950 (64 Stat. 306), the act of April 9, 1952 (66 Stat. 50), section 201 (e) (2) of the Immigration and Nationality Act, or any other act of Congress enacted prior to the date of the enactment of this act, be terminated effective July 1, 1957.

SECTION 9. ALIENS EXCLUDABLE BECAUSE OF CONVICTION OF CRIMINAL OFFENSES

Subsection (a) of section 9 (which is the same as section 9 of H. R. 8123) waives the provisions of paragraph (9) of section 212 (a) of the Immigration and Nationality Act in the case of an alien (1) who has a single conviction of an offense or offenses which, if committed in the United States would be classified as a misdemeanor or misdemeanors, each punishable by imprisonment not to exceed 1 year, if the fine or aggregate fines actually imposed for such conviction did not exceed $500, or for which the sentence or aggregate sentences to confinement actually imposed for such conviction did not exceed 6 months, or both, or (2) who has admitted to the commission of an offense or offenses, or the commission of acts constituting the essential elements of an offense or offenses which, if committed in the United States, would be a misdemeanor or misdemeanors punishable by imprisonment not to exceed 1 year.

Subsection (b) of such section waives the provisions of paragraph (9) of section 212 (a) of the Immigration and Nationality Act in the case of any alien who is the spouse, parent, or child of a United States citizen, or of an alien lawfully admitted for permanent residence, if the Attorney General believes that such alien's exclusion would result in extreme hardship to the United States citizen, or lawfully resident spouse, parent, or child of such alien and that such alien's admission would not be contrary to the national welfare, safety, or security of the United States.

SECTION 10. REPEAL OF SECTION 4 OF THE ACT OF SEPTEMBER 3, 1954

Section 10 (which is the same as section 10 of H. R. 8123) repeals section 4 of the act of September 3, 1954, which authorized the admission to the United States of an alien otherwise admissible but for the fact that such alien had been convicted of a misdemeanor, or had admitted to the Commission of a misdemeanor. This provision would be superseded by section 9 of the proposed amendment.

SECTION 11. ALIENS PAROLED INTO UNITED STATES

Section 11 (which is substantially the same as section 12 of S. 2222, introduced by Senator KENNEDY) authorizes aliens who are, or have been, paroled into the United States under section 212 (d) (5) of the Immigration and Nationality Act to apply for adjustment of status to that of an alien lawfully admitted for permanent residence.

If the Attorney General approves the application of an alien, he is required to submit a report thereon to the Congress. If either House then passes a resolution approving the adjustment of status of such alien, he will be required to depart from the United States in the manner provided by law. If neither House passes a resolution of disapproval, the alien will be regarded as having been lawfully admitted for permanent residence as of the date of his last entry into the United States.

SECTION 12. FINGERPRINTING

Section 12 (which is the same as section 6 of S. 129, introduced by Senator DIRKSEN) authorizes the Secretary of State and the Attorney General to waive, in the case of a nonimmigrant, the fingerprinting requirements contained in sections 221 (b) and 262 of the Immigration and Nationality Act.

SECTION 13. SPOUSE AND CHILDREN OF SPECIALLY SKILLED ALIENS

Section 13 (which is substantially the same as section 11 of S. 129) extends a quota immigrant status under section 203 (a) (1) (B) of the Immigration and Nationality Act to any alien who is following to join his spouse or parent who has been accorded a quota immigrant status under section 203 (a) (1) (A) (aliens whose services are urgently needed in the United States) and has been lawfully admitted to the United States for permanent residence.

SECTION 14. REPRESENTATIVES OF FOREIGN GOVERNMENTS—POLITICAL ASYLUM

Section 14 (which is substantially the same as section 13 of S. 129) authorizes an alien who (1) entered the United States as a representative, officer, or employee of a foreign government (including a representative to an international organization), or as a member of the household of such a representative, officer, or employee; (2) failed to maintain his status; and (3) has not been required to depart from the United States, to apply for adjustment of his status to that of an alien lawfully admitted for permanent residence.

If the Attorney General approves an application for adjustment of status, he is required to submit a report thereon to the Congress. If either House then passes a resolution disapproving the adjustment of status of such alien, he will be required to depart from the United States in the manner provided by law. If neither House passes a resolution of disapproval, the alien will be regarded as having been lawfully admitted for permanent residence as of the date of his last entry into the United States.

SECTION 15. UNUSED QUOTA NUMBERS

Section 15 (which is similar to section 5 of S. 129) authorizes the use of a portion of the unused quota numbers which remain unused at the end of each fiscal year. In general, each quota area (excluding quota areas having an annual quota in excess of 7,000) will receive that portion of the unused quota numbers which bears the same ratio to the total number of unused quota numbers as such quota area's annual quota bears to the total number of annual quota numbers. The Secretary of State is required to determine and announce, on or before October 1 following the close of each fiscal year, the number of unused quota numbers distributed to each quota area. Such quota numbers will be available for use for a period of 1 year (until the succeeding September 30), subject to the provisions of the Immigration and Nationality Act relating to eligibility for and issuance of immigrant visas.

During the first 2 years in which this section is in operation, quota numbers made

available by such section will be available for issuance, on a preferential basis, to aliens who applied for, and were qualified for, admission under the Refugee Relief Act of 1953, with respect to whom the necessary assurances required by that act had been made, and whose applications were being processed when the time for issuing visas under that act expired. The quota numbers which would otherwise be distributed to each quota area as explained in the preceding paragraph will be proportionately reduced during these 2 years.

SECTION 16. DEFINITIONS

Section 16 (which is the same as section 11 of H. R. 8123) provides that the definitions contained in sections 101 (a) and (b) of the Immigration and Nationality Act shall apply to terms used in the proposed amendment.

Mr. KENNEDY. Mr. President, on June 5, 1957, I introduced a bill; S. 2222, which addressed itself to what I feel are emergency immigration problems which require the attention of the Congress during the present session. One of the prime purposes of S. 2222 was to bring about the reunion of families and enable the United States to assume a fair share of the responsibility to resettle refugees and escapees from Communist-dominated countries. There have been other bills introduced before and since which approach certain other aspects of our current immigration policy. Most notable among these was H. R. 8123, introduced by the distinguished Representative from Pennsylvania, Mr. WALTER. H. R. 8123 contained many provisions similar to those in S. 2222, but it went further in making technical and other improvements to alleviate hardship under the act.

After carefully examining Mr. WALTER's bill and conferring with many of our colleagues, especially the distinguished majority leader [Mr. JOHNSON], we concluded that a combination of bills embracing the best features of all of them was the best solution. The bill which we are introducing represents that combination.

I wish to reiterate to my colleagues in the Senate that this bill has been carefully drafted after thoughtful consideration and discussion by many Members in both Houses of Congress. The distinguished Representative from Pennsylvania, Mr. WALTER, has assured me that the major provisions of the bill are in accord with his thinking on the subject and that it has his strong support.

This bill is a strong bill, and one which no Member of this body need feel any hesitancy in supporting. It is a carefully worked out, yet simple, measure which would afford immediate relief to pressing problems and provides a better utilization of now unused quotas in the future.

Since a full analysis will be available, I shall just briefly state that this bill would reunite families, provide for better utilization of currently available quotas which go unused each year, remove the mortgages on existing quotas which have been imposed by past acts of Congress. Further, the bill would admit orphans adopted by United States citizens, forgive certain misrepresentations which are grounds for deportation of

aliens already here, admit members of families who suffer from tuberculosis under careful safeguards so as to protect the health of our own citizens, provide a limited number of visas for refugees who constitute serious moral economic and political problems.

This is not an exhaustive list of the provisions of the bill and I trust that every Senator will study the bill carefully. I am confident that, with the strong support this bill already has and because of the intrinsic merit of the bill, it can and should receive favorable consideration during the present session.

Mr. PASTORE. Mr. President, I am happy to add my sponsorship to the bill introduced by the Senator from Massachusetts [Mr. KENNEDY]. The bill does not represent the maximum of our desires, but it is an important step forward in the interests of mercy and justice in a disturbed world.

We will continue to press forward, but having in mind at all times the best interests of America.

No one can ever say he has done the last final act in an immigration policy because no one knows the events of tomorrow or the crisis of the day after. What this measure seeks to do is to alleviate some of the family tragedies that arise through the very earnestness of these United States in meeting emergencies. It would unite separated families and give consideration to orphans who have the promise of loving homes in America. It would help a small number who find themselves homeless and stateless in the cataclysm of their former world. It would apply American standards to cases that call for equity and justice. It would not open the gates to a greater number of immigrants than these United States have calculated they can absorb.

The measure is not omniscient, but it is important in these difficult times. It is a gesture of friendship when the United States emphasizes its desire to be friends with a peace-seeking world.

It is my fervent hope that the Senate Judiciary Committee will give this measure immediate attention, and will take favorable action on it.

Mr. HUMPHREY. Mr. President, I wish to commend the Senator from Massachusetts [Mr. KENNEDY], the Senator from Rhode Island [Mr. PASTORE], and the Senator from Ohio [Mr. LAUSCHE] on the introduction of this very important measure. I have just asked the distinguished Senator from Massachusetts whether he will permit me to join him in the sponsorship of the bill, in view of my interest in immigration measures. He has kindly acceded to that request. I am delighted to be able to associate myself with the sponsorship of the bill. Its provisions are much needed. It is our hope that action on the bill will be expedited. Enactment of the bill will mean a forward step in the field of immigration legislation.

ORDER OF BUSINESS

Mr. MANSFIELD. Mr. President, has morning business been concluded?

The PRESIDING OFFICER (Mr. NEUBERGER in the chair). Is there further morning business?

Mr. HUMPHREY. Mr. President, I understand the Senator from Arizona had a measure which he wanted to have considered. I do not want to interfere with that procedure but I should like to have the floor following the statement of the Senator from Arizona and action on the measure he wishes to have considered.

Mr. MANSFIELD. Mr. President, I ask unanimous consent that that privilege may be accorded the Senator from Minnesota.

The PRESIDING OFFICER. Is there objection? The Chair hears none, and it is so ordered.

Mr. MANSFIELD. Mr. President, I take it morning business is concluded.

The PRESIDING OFFICER. Is there further morning business? If not, morning business is closed.

Mr. MANSFIELD. Mr. President, what is the pending business?

The PRESIDING OFFICER. The Chair is informed that the pending business will not come automatically before the Senate until 2 o'clock, although it can be taken up by motion.

STOCKPILE OF EXTRA LONG STAPLE COTTON

Mr. MANSFIELD. Mr. President, I ask unanimous consent that Calendar No. 470, House Joint Resolution 172, which would automatically become the pending business at 2 o'clock, be made the pending business at this time, 1:17 o'clock p. m.

The PRESIDING OFFICER. Is there objection to the unanimous-consent request? If not, the Chair lays before the Senate the pending business.

The Senate resumed the consideration of the joint resolution (H. J. Res. 172) relating to the stockpile of extra long staple cotton under the Strategic and Critical Materials Stockpiling Act.

Mr. GOLDWATER. Mr. President, this joint resolution which has come from the House is similar to one my senior colleague from Arizona [Mr. HAYDEN] and I introduced in the Senate this year. We have yielded to the House version. All the bill does is allow 50,000 bales of surplus cotton held in stockpile by the Office of Defense Mobilization to be released to the market. At the present time there is a scarcity of long staple cotton. The mills are crying for it. We should like this done so the price of cotton will not go so high as to injure planters of long staple cotton in the West.

There was a question as to whether such cotton would be counted as a part of the carryover immediately after the enactment of House Joint Resolution 172 while still owned by the Federal Government, or whether it would count only after being sold into the private trade by the disposal agency of the Government.

Mr. President, I ask unanimous consent that a letter I addressed to the Honorable Ezra T. Benson, Secretary of Agriculture, and his reply on the question be printed at this point in the RECORD.

There being no objection, the letters were ordered to be printed in the RECORD, as follows:

JUNE 19, 1957.

The Honorable EZRA T. BENSON,
Secretary of Agriculture,
Department of Agriculture,
Washington, D. C.

MY DEAR MR. SECRETARY: The Senate Committee on Agriculture and Forestry reported favorably without amendment, House Joint Resolution 172, which provides for the release of 50,000 bales of United States-grown extra-long-staple cotton from the strategic and critical materials stockpile. I introduced for myself and on behalf of Senator HAYDEN, a companion measure, Senate Joint Resolution 63. Accordingly, I am very much interested in this matter.

The question has arisen as to whether such cotton would be counted as a part of the carryover immediately after the enactment of House Joint Resolution 172, while still owned by the Federal Government, or whether it would count only after being sold into the private trade by the disposing agency of the Government. The committee report contains the following paragraph with respect to this question:

"Section 301' (d) of the Agricultural Adjustment Act of 1938 provides as follows:

" '(d) In making any determination under that act or under the Agricultural Act of 1949 with respect to the carryover of any agricultural commodity, the Secretary shall exclude from such determination the stocks of any commodity acquired pursuant to, or under the authority of, the Strategic and Critical Materials Stock Piling Act (60 Stat. 596) (7 U. S. C. 1301 (d)).'"

So long as this cotton remains in the stockpile it is clear that it would not be counted as a part of the carryover, even though it were available for sale under section 3 of the Stock Piling Act. However, some question has arisen as to whether the provision of the joint resolution that the cotton be withdrawn and transferred to the Commodity Credit Corporation would remove this cotton from the provision of section 301 (d). There is no such intention. The cotton would remain subject to section 301 (d), whether held by one agency of the Government or another and will not be counted as part of the carryover so long as it is held by the Commodity Credit Corporation.

I would appreciate your advising me whether the Department will clarify the 50,000 bales of long-staple cotton in accordance with the above-quoted paragraph of the committee report, or whether there is no legislative history developed to the contrary during consideration of House Joint Resolution 172 by the Senate.

This is a matter of great importance to the producers of extra-long-staple cotton in Arizona as well as the other producing States. I would appreciate an immediate answer, as I would like to have your reply when the measure is considered by the Senate.

Sincerely,

BARRY GOLDWATER.

DEPARTMENT OF AGRICULTURE,
Washington, D. C., June 24, 1957.

Hon. BARRY GOLDWATER,
United States Senate.

DEAR SENATOR GOLDWATER: This is in reply to your letter of June 19, 1957, informing us that the Senate Committee on Agriculture and Forestry reported favorably without amendment House Joint Resolution 172 which provides for the release of 50,000 bales of United States grown extra-long-staple cotton from the strategic and critical materials stockpile.

We note in consideration of this resolution the question arose as to whether such

cotton would be counted as a part of the carryover immediately after the enactment of House Joint Resolution 172 while still owned by the Federal Government or whether it will count only after being sold into private trade by the disposing agency of the Government. We further note a paragraph was inserted in the committee report in order to make clear that the cotton should not be counted in the carryover until it was disposed of by the Government. With the wording quoted in your letter in the committee report and if there is no legislative history developed to the contrary in consideration of the resolution, it would be clear that it was the intention of the Congress that the cotton in question should only be considered in the carryover after it has been sold by the disposing agency of the Government and the statute would be so construed by this Department.

Sincerely yours.

MARVIN L. McLAIN,
Assistant Secretary.

Mr. HAYDEN. Mr. President, the Senator from Mississippi [Mr. EASTLAND], who reported the bill to the Senate, requested me to make a statement for him in his absence. I am glad to do so.

House Joint Resolution 172 provides for the transfer to, and sale by, Commodity Credit Corporation of 50,000 bales of extra-long-staple cotton now in the stockpile established pursuant to the Strategic and Critical Materials Stock Piling Act. The Office of Defense Mobilization recently concluded that present inventories of long-staple cotton should be sold; but the Stock Piling Act requires 6 months' notice prior to sale. The effect of the resolution will therefore be to waive the 6 months' notice with regard to 50,000 bales. There is a current shortage of this type of cotton, and in order to protect producers, processors, and consumers, and minimize the United States' loss, the cotton should be made available now, while the shortage exists, rather than after the new crop becomes available in October.

The Department of Agriculture advised on April 9 that the cotton in the stockpile was acquired at prices averaging about $1.05 a pound, and could then be sold at about 63 cents a pound, for a loss of about $10,500,000. Since then the price has weakened somewhat, so that prompt passage of the resolution is needed to avert further loss. Passage of the resolution will therefore result in no increase in expenditures, but will reduce expenditures for storage charges and avert further loss.

The PRESIDING OFFICER (Mr. LAUSCHE in the chair). The joint resolution is open to amendment. If there be no amendment to be proposed, the question is on the third reading of the joint resolution.

The joint resolution (H. J. Res. 172) was ordered to a third reading, read the third time, and passed.

RISING INTEREST RATES

Mr. HUMPHREY. Mr. President, although I know how painful it is to my Republican colleagues to have anyone bring up the subject of rising interest rates and the fiscal dilemma of the Treasury, I feel bound in good conscience to keep the record up to date.

Each Monday the Wall Street Journal reports the Dow-Jones municipal yield index. This past Monday it reported that quotations on municipal bonds dropped again—for the fifth straight week, I might add—to 3.46 percent. This is a 22-year low. I ask unanimous consent, Mr. President, that this report of June 17 in the Wall Street Journal appear in the RECORD at this point of my remarks.

There being no objection, the article was ordered to be printed in the RECORD, as follows:

TAX-EXEMPTS: PRICE DROP LAST WEEK CARRIED MUNICIPAL TO NEW 22-YEAR LOWS

Quotations on tax-exempt municipal bonds slipped to their lowest levels in nearly 22 years last week, as dealers marked down older issues in their inventory to bring them in line with new issues coming into the market.

The Dow-Jones municipal yield index, which moves inversely to prices, now reads 3.46 percent, up from 3.43 percent last Monday. It was the fifth consecutive week marked by price deterioration for tax-exempt securities. The last time municipal bond yields were as high as at present was in October 1935, when the index of 20-year issues read 3.50 percent.

As has been the case previously, last week's markdowns in municipal bond quotations were accompanied by declining prices for United States Government securities. The two longest United States Treasury issues reached their lowest prices on record.

But the municipal bond scene was not devoid of its encouraging aspects, traders said. New issues went well at retail and dealers were able to point to other factors indicating the tax-exempts market is working toward an improved technical position. Notable among these is the further reduction in the shelf-supply and the continued limited volume of new issues scheduled for early sale.

As reported by the Blue List, the advertised supply of tax-exempt securities undistributed with dealers stands at $208,368,000. That is down from $227,921,500 last Monday, and from $275,820,000 3 weeks ago. New municipal offerings in sight for the next 30 days amount to a moderate $175,088,887, according to the Daily Bond Buyer.

Retail successes chalked up in the more active market included Ohio's $32 million of road bonds, and Cowlitz County, Wash., $20.3 million of electric system revenue obligations—the week's two largest issues. Both offerings sold out quickly, a fact cited by some dealers as evidence there is "money around to buy tax-exempt bonds at prevailing price levels."

This week's limited $69,507,308 tax-exempt bond offering schedule is topped by State of Vermont's $9,300,000 various purpose issue on Thursday.

Mr. HUMPHREY. Mr. President, on Tuesday of this week the Treasury announced that 91-day bills which were offered June 13 jumped to a rate of 3.404 percent, the highest level since the "bank holiday" in 1933. I ask unanimous consent that this story from the Wall Street Journal of June 18 appear at this point in my remarks in the RECORD.

There being no objection, the article was ordered to be printed in the RECORD, as follows:

TREASURY BILL RATE RISES TO 3.404 PERCENT, HIGHEST SINCE 1933 BANK HOLIDAY

WASHINGTON.—The Treasury's short-term borrowing costs jumped to 3.404 percent—the highest level since the "bank holiday" period of 1933.

At the time of the bank moratorium, the Treasury paid more than 4 percent to borrow short-term money. The highest rate since then had been the 3.374 percent paid 2 weeks ago.

Last week the 91-day Treasury bill rate dipped to 3,256 percent. But this week the rate turned up again to a new 24-year high. Last year in mid-June the Treasury sold short-term bills at 2.430 percent.

The Treasury's interest cost on 91-day bills is considered a key indicator of short-term money market conditions. A rising rate indicates the cost of short-term money is becoming more expensive. The Senate Finance Committee, headed by Senator BYRD, Democrat, of Virginia, today begins an investigation into the administration's so-called "tight" money policies that some Democrats claim have caused high interest rates.

At its current level, the Treasury bill rate now tops the 3-percent discount rate charged by the Federal Reserve System on loans to member banks by a substantial margin.

The Reserve Board is known to be considering another boost in the system's discount rate. Chairman Martin recently described inflationary forces in the economy as still "formidable." Also, the Board's latest report on business conditions in May noted interest rates had risen "substantially."

However, the Treasury is expected to be in the market soon to borrow funds to meet its cash needs for July, when tax receipts are seasonally low. This would tend to dissuade the Reserve Board from raising its discount rate since the Board prefers not to upset the market while the Treasury is financing.

On the issue, accepted bids ranged from a high of 99.160 (3.322 percent), to a low of 93.128 (3.418 percent), and an average price of 99.139 (3.404 percent). Of the amount bid for at the low price, 65 percent was accepted, the Treasury said.

Applications for the issue aggregated $2,444,049,000. The Treasury accepted $1,- 600,299,000, including $373,999,000 offered on a noncompetitive basis and accepted in full at the average price.

These bills are dated June 20, and mature September 19, 1957.

Mr. HUMPHREY. Each day seems to bring new reports of soaring interest rates. This past Wednesday, it was announced that Southern Bell Telephone & Telegraph Co. had to pay 4.91 percent for the $70 million it raised on 29-year debentures. This is the costliest rate this company has had to pay since October 18, 1929, when it sold $32 million of 5-percent bonds at 5.32 percent. I ask unanimous consent that an article spelling out the details on this transaction from the June 19 issue of the Wall Street Journal be printed in the RECORD at this point in my remarks.

There being no objection, the article was ordered to be printed in the RECORD, as follows:

SOUTHERN BELL $70 MILLION ISSUE SOLD AT 4.91-PERCENT RATE—BORROWING COST ON 29-YEAR DEBENTURES IS HIGHEST FOR THE UTILITY SINCE 1929—BIG RETAIL DEMAND REPORTED

NEW YORK.—Southern Bell Telephone & Telegraph Co. will pay 4.91 percent annually for the $70 million it raised on 29-year debentures.

That marks the borrowing as the costliest for Southern Bell since October 18, 1929, when it sold $32 million of 5-percent bonds at 5.32 percent.

It also ranks as the most expensive debt financing by any Bell System unit since January 13, 1930, when parent A. T. & T. itself floated $150 million of 5-percent debentures at a cost of 5.22 percent.

Yesterday's lofty rate came about notwithstanding the fact that Southern Bell agreed to make the 29-year securities noncallable for the first 5 years.

Halsey, Stuart & Co. Inc., and associates won the big issue with a bid of 101.33 for a 5-percent coupon.

Following compliance with Securities and Exchange Commission requirements, the group is putting the debentures out for general distribution at 102.32, to yield 4.85 percent to maturity on June 1, 1986.

An unmistakably big retail demand for the securities at this price was building up, ahead of today's formal public offering.

A closely competing bid of 101.20 for the debentures as 5's came from a Morgan Stanley & Co. group.

Yesterday's 4.91 percent net interest cost compares with 3.95 percent Southern Bell is paying for the $60 million it raised last October 8 on 27-year debenture 4s.

Southern Bell will use the proceeds from the new issue, President Ben S. Gilmer said, "to provide telephone facilities to meet the continuing strong demand for telephone service in the South."

Mr. HUMPHREY. Mr. President, in a recent issue of the Washington Post and Times Herald there appeared two very interesting items concerning the present but soon departing Secretary of the Treasury George Humphrey. One story reports on the stock holdings of Secretary Humphrey as of January, 1953; according to the computation that has been made these stock holdings were then worth more than $7 million. Based on yesterday's closing prices, these same stocks are now worth approximately $12 million. That is not a bad record for only four years. Imagine that, Mr. President. An increase of almost $5 million in the value of the Secretary's 1953 stock holdings. After paying the capital gains tax his profits would amount to roughly $3.75 million. The Secretary's stock has increased in value by 71 percent and after taxes he would have a gain of around 50 percent.

However, as the Secretary pointed out to the Finance Committee on Tuesday, this glorious Republican prosperity has benefited us all. For example, the Secretary noted that workers' take home pay has risen about $10 a week, a little more than 15 percent. The workers get $10 a week and the Secretary realizes a net gain of almost $20,000 a week. I repeat, Mr. President, $20,000 a week.

I ask unanimous consent that this story on the Secretary's stock earnings in the June 20 issue of the Washington Post and Times Herald be printed in the RECORD at this point in my remarks.

There being no objection, the article was ordered to be printed in the RECORD, as follows:

LIST OF STOCKHOLDINGS SUBMITTED BY HUMPHREY

Secretary of the Treasury George M. Humphrey yesterday submitted to the Senate Finance Committee a list of his stock holdings at the time he entered the Cabinet. A computation showed the holdings were worth more than $7 million in January 1953.

Based on yesterday's closing prices, the quoted value of the holdings would be approximately $12 million.

Chairman HARRY F. BYRD, Democrat, of Virginia, made the list public at once. He said Humphrey offered the information "gladly and cheerfully." It was placed in the hear-

ing record of the Committee's inquiry into the Nation's financial condition.

VALUE NOT GIVEN

Humphrey gave the number of shares of various corporations he owned as of Jan. 12, 1953, but not the value of the stocks. Based on the closing prices of all but one of the issues at the time, the total amounted to $7,093,906. Humphrey said he had sold his holdings in the National City Bank of Cleveland. There was no announcement as to whether he still holds the remaining securities.

Senator ALBERT GORE, Democrat, of Tennessee, had raised the point that the list of holdings, first given to the Committee in 1953 but not made public then, was missing from the files.

BYRD yesterday conceded this was correct but said Humphrey had offered to supply the list anew.

Gore had said previously he would question Humphrey about his holdings now to show how his financial status has changed during his stay in Washington. However, the Tennessee Senator's turn for questioning is not expected to come for several days.

HOLDINGS ON JANUARY 12, 1953

Following is a list of Humphrey's holdings on January 12, 1953, and the values at that time as closely as could be computed:

Pittsburgh Consolidation Coal Co., 20,000 shares of common, at $56.72 a share—$1,- 135,000.

National Steel Corp., 13,200 shares of capital stock, at $50 a share—$760,000.

Republic Steel Corp., 120 shares of common, at $45.75 a share—$5,490.

The above totals are based on closing prices of the issues on the New York Stock Exchange on Monday, January 12, 1953.

The following are based on the bid and asked prices of over-the-counter stocks on Friday, January 2, 1953:

Canada & Dominion Sugar Co., Ltd., 100 shares of capital stock, $16.62 bid, $17.12 asked—$1,662.

The M. A. Hanna Co., 44,550 shares of Class A common, $76 bid $78 asked—$3,- 385,800.

The M. A. Hanna Co., 23,000 shares of Class B common stock, $76 bid, $80 asked—$1,- 794,000.

The National City Bank of Cleveland, 278 shares of common, $43 bid, $44 asked—$11,- 954.

The list also included Hanna Coal & Ore Corp., 12,471.3 shares of common stock. It was not immediately possible to determine the value of these holdings, as the stock is not traded on the exchanges.

Mr. HUMPHREY. Mr. President, another item I wish to mention today is a letter to the editor in the Washington Post and Times Herald. It is titled "Mr. Humphrey's Legacy: A Critical Appraisal" and is written by Seymour Harris, chairman of the department of economics of Harvard University. Perhaps I should state that the "Mr. Humphrey" referred to is Secretary George Humphrey and not the junior Senator from Minnesota. I ask unanimous consent that this letter to the editor be printed in the RECORD at this point in my remarks.

There being no objection, the letter to the editor was ordered to be printed in the RECORD, as follows:

MR. HUMPHREY'S LEGACY: A CRITICAL APPRAISAL

The press almost universally has greeted Secretary Humphrey's announced departure from public life with encomium. Indeed, the Secretary has many virtues: he is smart, shrewd, persuasive, aggressive, hard working,

There being no objection, the article was ordered to be printed in the RECORD, as follows:

SOUTHERN BELL $70 MILLION ISSUE SOLD AT 4.91-PERCENT RATE—BORROWING COST ON 29-YEAR DEBENTURES IS HIGHEST FOR THE UTILITY SINCE 1929—BIG RETAIL DEMAND REPORTED

NEW YORK.—Southern Bell Telephone & Telegraph Co. will pay 4.91 percent annually for the $70 million it raised on 29-year debentures.

That marks the borrowing as the costliest for Southern Bell since October 18, 1929, when it sold $32 million of 5-percent bonds at 5.32 percent.

It also ranks as the most expensive debt financing by any Bell System unit since January 13, 1930, when parent A. T. & T. itself floated $150 million of 5-percent debentures at a cost of 5.22 percent.

Post and Times Herald be printed in the RECORD at this point in my remarks.

There being no objection, the article was ordered to be printed in the RECORD, as follows:

LIST OF STOCKHOLDINGS SUBMITTED BY HUMPHREY

Secretary of the Treasury George M. Humphrey yesterday submitted to the Senate Finance Committee a list of his stock holdings at the time he entered the Cabinet. A computation showed the holdings were worth more than $7 million in January 1953.

Based on yesterday's closing prices, the quoted value of the holdings would be approximately $12 million.

Chairman HARRY F. BYRD, Democrat, of Virginia, made the list public at once. He said Humphrey offered the information "gladly and cheerfully." It was placed in the hear-

al" and is written by Seymour Harris, chairman of the department of economics of Harvard University. Perhaps I should state that the "Mr. Humphrey" referred to is Secretary George Humphrey and not the junior Senator from Minnesota. I ask unanimous consent that this letter to the editor be printed in the RECORD at this point in my remarks.

There being no objection, the letter to the editor was ordered to be printed in the RECORD, as follows:

MR. HUMPHREY'S LEGACY: A CRITICAL APPRAISAL

The press almost universally has greeted Secretary Humphrey's announced departure from public life with encomium. Indeed, the Secretary has many virtues: he is smart, shrewd, persuasive, aggressive, hard working,

Public Law 85-96
85th Congress, H. J. Res. 172
July 10, 1957

JOINT RESOLUTION

71 Stat. 290.

Relating to the stockpile of extra long staple cotton under the Strategic and
Critical Materials Stockpiling Act.

Resolved by the Senate and House of Representatives of the United
States of America in Congress assembled, That notwithstanding any
other provision of law, fifty thousand bales of domestically grown
extra long staple cotton in the stockpile (including any cotton which
does not meet current stockpile specifications) established pursuant
to the Strategic and Critical Materials Stockpiling Act, as amended
(50 U. S. C. 98), shall be withdrawn and transferred to the Commodity Credit Corporation for sale at not less than the prices at
which the Commodity Credit Corporation may sell its stocks under the
minimum pricing provision of section 407 of the Agricultural Act of
1949, as amended. Proceeds from such sale, less costs incurred by
Commodity Credit Corporation, including administrative expense, as
determined by the Secretary of Agriculture, shall be covered into the
Treasury of the United States as miscellaneous receipts.

Approved July 10, 1957.

Cotton.
Withdrawal
from stock-
pile.

60 Stat. 596.
50 USC 98 note.

63 Stat. 1055;
70 Stat. 6.
7 USC 1427.

GPO 84139

There being no objection, the arti
was ordered to be printed in the Reco
as follows:

SOUTHERN BELL $70 MILLION ISSUE SOLD
4.31-PERCENT RATE—BORROWING COST
29-YEAR DEBENTURES IS HIGHEST FOR 1
UTILITY SINCE 1929—BIG RETAIL DEMA
REPORTED